Development, the International Economic Order, and Commodity Agreements

Jere R. Behrman
University of Pennsylvania

ADDISON-WESLEY PUBLISHING COMPANY
Reading, Massachusetts • Menlo Park, California
London • Amsterdam • Don Mills, Ontario • Sydney

PERSPECTIVES ON ECONOMICS SERIES

Michael L. Wachter & Susan M. Wachter, Editors

PUBLISHED

**Development, The International Economic Order
and Commodity Agreements,** *Jere R. Behrman*
**The Economics of Medical Care:
A Policy Perspective,** *Joseph P. Newhouse*
Money and Economy: A Monetarist View, *William Poole*
Antitrust Policies and Issues, *Roger Sherman*
Income Distribution and Redistribution, *Paul J. Taubman*

AVAILABLE IN LATE 1978 AND EARLY 1979

Labor Unions, *George H. Hildebrand*
Forecasting, *Lawrence R. Klein & Richard M. Young*
International Trade, *Stephen P. Magee*
Regulation, *Roger G. Noll*
Population, *T. Paul Schultz*
Urban Economics, *Susan M. Wachter*

ISBN 0-201-08367-1
ABCDEFGHIJK-AL-798

Foreword

The PERSPECTIVES ON ECONOMICS series has been developed to present economics students with up-to-date policy-oriented books written by leading scholars in this field. Many professors and students have stressed the need for flexible, contemporary materials that provide an understanding of current policy issues.

In general, beginning students in economics are not exposed to the controversial material and development of current issues that are the basis of research in economics. Because of their length and breadth of coverage, textbooks tend to lack current economic thinking on policy questions; in attempting to provide a balanced viewpoint, they often do not give the reader a feel for the lively controversy in each field. With this series, we have attempted to fill this void.

The books in this series are designed to complement standard textbooks. Each volume reflects the research interests and views of the authors. Thus these books can also serve as basic reading material in the specific topic courses covered by each. The stress throughout is on the careful development of institutional factors and policy in the context of economic theory. Yet the exposition is designed bo be accessible to undergraduate students and interested laypersons with an elementary background in economics.

Michael L. Wachter
Susan M. Wachter

Preface

Hundreds of millions of persons live in great poverty in Asia, Africa, Latin America, and other parts of the developing world. The major economic problem of the last quarter of the twentieth century, in my view, is how to raise them from current levels of abysmal poverty.

The major point of economic contact between the developing nations and developed countries such as the United States is through international markets. The developing nations depend on their export of primary commodities for the majority of their foreign exchange, which they need for critical food and machinery imports.

In recent years the developing nations have become ever more frustrated with "the rules of the game" for international economic transactions. They perceive that these rules were established by the developed countries with their own interests primarily in mind. Therefore, in 1974 the developing nations joined in a call for a new international economic order. At the heart of this call is a system of international commodity agreements, which were codified in the UNCTAD (United Nations Committee on Trade and Development) Integrated Commodity Program of 1976. This proposal is now being considered in international forums.

If the UNCTAD proposal, or some modified version thereof, is adopted, the impact on international economic trade and on the developing nations alike may be very substantial—perhaps on the order of magnitude of the OPEC oil arrangements. However, there is considerable controversy about the probable effects of this proposal.

This book clarifies the issues involved by analyzing international commodity proposals for the UNCTAD ten core commodities and basic foodgrains. To provide perspective, the first two chapters discuss the nature of development goals, analysis of the development process, the role of international trade in that process, and events that led up to the call for a new international economic order. The rest of the book focuses on the analysis of the UNCTAD integrated commodity program that is the key to that call. Three basic modes of analysis are used: (1) simple economic theory, (2) examination of historical experience, and (3) simulation of what would happen if the proposed agreements were implemented, given estimated dynamic models of the relevant international markets. This analysis is explained sufficiently so that the book is self-contained and understandable to intelligent laypersons and students in introductory economics courses, with substantial reinforcement for the latter group of the knowledge gained in their course work. More technical material for particularly interested readers is given in two appendixes. The use of alternative analytical modes promotes understanding of the issues at hand and points to the strengths and weaknesses of the various approaches. The conclusions are qualified, but suggest that there may be substantial gains to both developing and developed nations if the proposed agreements are implemented—a conclusion in contrast to the assertions of many economists and policymakers in the United States.

Thus this study illustrates how economists analyze problems and policies. To do so it considers not some sterile abstractions, but a very important real-world problem, with far-reaching implications for people all over the globe. Thereby the analysis is much more germane and alive than is normally encountered in economics texts and readers. It is hoped that diligent readers will be amply rewarded for their efforts.

Philadelphia, Pennsylvania   J. R. B.
March 1978

Contents

Introduction: 1
The Economic
Development Problem
and International
Commodity Markets

International organizations often divide the world into three groups: the developed market economies, with about 18 percent of world population and 66 percent of world product; the centrally planned economies, with about 32 percent of world population and 20 percent of world product; and the developing countries, with over half of world population and 14 percent of world product.[1] Countries in the last group are also frequently referred to as the underdeveloped countries, the less developed countries (LDCs), or the Third World. This group includes over two billion people, many of whom experience relatively great poverty.

In the modern era of the past several centuries, much of the population in the developed market economies and some of the population in the centrally planned economies has experienced economic growth of previously unprecedented magnitudes. In contrast, most of the population in the developing countries has continued to live in poverty or, in some cases, has become more impoverished. Literally hundreds of millions of persons currently live in squalor in these lands, with constant illness, near-starvation diets, crowded living quarters, almost no sanitation, and effectively no control over their own destinies.

---

1 The developed market economies include most of Western Europe, the United States, Canada, Japan, Australia, South Africa, and New Zealand. The centrally-planned economies include most of Eastern Europe, the People's Republic of China, Cuba, Mongolia, and the Democratic Republics of Korea and Vietnam. The developing countries are the rest of the countries in the world, primarily in Africa, Asia, and Latin America. Current world population is about four billion people. Current world gross national product is about five trillion United States dollars. The World Bank Group [1] is a good source for country and regional data on population, product, and growth rates.

In recent years, criticism of further economic growth in the developed nations has become quite widespread because of perceived negative effects of that growth on the environment and on human relations and because of the perceived failure of that growth to lead to the resolution of many important social problems. At the same time, criticisms of the traditional patterns of growth in the developing countries have also arisen because of the widespread failure to improve the economic situation of the poorest in those lands.

Depending on your value judgments and your perceptions of reality, you may concur with many of these criticisms. I do. And yet, while I am able to raise many questions about past economic policies and patterns in the developing countries, I am forced by the stark reality of the miserable existence of hundreds of millions of persons to see the major economic problem of the world in the last quarter of the twentieth century to be the elevation of those individuals and of their children out of extreme poverty. Whether or not their subsequent economic development should reflect elements of the experience of the present developed market and centrally planned economies is debatable. But what is essential is the movement of this large portion of humanity to an existence in which they have some element of choice about their life instead of constantly being overwhelmed by grinding poverty. Such economic development, in my judgment, overshadows all other economic problems.

How can such development take place? Considerable dispute exists in regard to this question. We review some of these issues below. Much of the answer probably resides in substantial transformations within the developing lands.

But another important factor affecting the options of the LDCs is the external economic situation in which they must operate. And this external situation is the part of their economic reality that is most subject to policy decisions of the developed market economies, including the United States, and of the centrally planned nations.

This book is concerned with the analysis of important policy issues related to economic interactions between the developing countries and the other two groups. Because of their dissatisfaction with the nature of such relations historically, the developing countries recently have issued a call for a "new international economic order." At the heart of this call is a proposal for international commodity agreements. Their proposals for change are far ranging. They may have important implications throughout the rest of the twentieth century not only for the hundreds of millions of people in the developing countries, but also for consumers of coffee, copper, and other primary commodities in the United States and throughout the rest of the world. Thus the subject of this book may have substantial and widespread ramifications.

The rest of this chapter provides some perspective about the general question of economic development and the role of international trade in that process. Section 1.1 discusses major economic goals. Section 1.2 considers what we know about the causes of economic development. Section 1.3 examines the role of foreign trade in the development process. Section 1.4 presents conclusions.

To provide further perspective, Chapter 2 reviews the recent experience of the developing nations and the call for a new international economic order. The rest of the book analyzes some of the major changes proposed for primary raw material and foodgrain international trade, which are at the heart of the call for a new international economic order. To illustrate how economists explore important policy issues and to help you understand the implications of the proposed changes in international trade, we have used three modes of analysis: economic theory, consideration of the historical experience of efforts to regulate international commodity markets, and simulations of what would happen if the proposed changes were implemented. The general conclusion of this examination is that the developing and developed countries alike might gain significantly from the implementation of the proposed changes in international commodity markets—despite claims to the contrary by many analysts in the developed world. Both developing and developed nations should explore seriously the programs being proposed. While such changes would increase the options of the developing world, however, they should not be viewed as a panacea. Nor should it be presumed that the poorest members of the LDC populations would automatically benefit.

1.1 MAJOR ECONOMIC DEVELOPMENT GOALS

The developing countries vary enormously in size, natural and human resource endowments, degree of integration into world markets, types of social and political systems, degrees of urbanization, cultural homogeneity, religion, and other pertinent characteristics. Despite such diversity, on a very general level there is a widely shared desire for development in order to increase the welfare of their populations on a sustained basis.

Such a goal, however, is very broad. It requires knowledge about what determines welfare, which strictly speaking is difficult, if not impossible, to obtain. Therefore development economists traditionally have focused upon the goal of attaining sustained growth in per capita income. For most of the developing countries (although there are a few exceptions, primarily among the smallest oil rich nations), per capita income levels are low in comparison to those prevalent in the developed market economies. The population and product distributions cited at the start of this chapter, for example, imply that the average per capita product in the developing countries is $350 per year, less than 8 percent of the average in the developed market economies. In 1973 almost one billion persons lived in developing countries with average per capita products of no more than $150, as compared to an average of $6,200 for the United States. To understand what this means, ask yourself how you would fare on $2 or $3 per week, then realize that hundreds of millions of people in the developing nations are existing on less than that.[2]

In the first two decades after the Second World War, the majority of development economists tended to focus primarily, and at times exclusively, on the goal of increasing average product per capita. As is noted above, this degree of focus has recently been criticized from several viewpoints:

1. It is alleged (and documented in some, but not all, cases) that growth in average income has been accompanied by a worsening of the relative—and perhaps even the absolute—position of the poorest member of society. Therefore the distribution of income (or of wealth) should be incorporated as an explicit goal.

2. A related concern is with labor employment and dualism. Dualism is the existence of a small, relatively modern sector with relatively heavy use of machinery and equipment and high product per worker, alongside of a large traditional sector with limited use of machinery and equipment, low product per worker, and a large number of unemployed workers. Perhaps such dualism is inevitable as part of the development process. But recent critics have argued otherwise. They maintain that productive employment is very important in order to develop human potentialities and social consciousness. Therefore employment should be included as a separate end in itself, not just the concomitant of growth in product. To make possible widespread productive employment and to avoid dualism, the argument continues, new intermediate technology, with less machinery and equipment per worker than in the modern sector, but more productivity than in the traditional sector, must be developed.[3]

3. Another important dimension is the existence of shortrun instability problems. These may be classified into three types: (1) instability in real terms, which results in unused productive capacity (such as being at point C in Fig. 1.1); (2) instability in nominal terms or inflation; and (3) instability in the balance of payments with the rest of the world, payments which are

---

2 Careful comparisons of the actual prices paid for purchases in developing nations indicate that the above figures (obtained by using official exchange rates to translate from other currencies into dollars) overstate the relative poverty of the developing nations. But even if they are off by 200 or 300 percent, very low levels of income are indicated. How would you fare on $2-$3 per week merely becomes how would you fare on $4-$12 per week?

3 For a very readable nontechnical statement of this position, see Schumacher [2].

necessary for international trade and financial movements. The first of these results in lower output, income, and development of human resources, as is discussed below. The second tends to cause distortions, unintended shifts in real income, increased transaction costs, and rewards for behavior that may not be very productive from a social point of view. The third may restrain imports of important final goods (for example, basic consumption goods or machinery and equipment) and intermediate inputs (for example, petroleum) and thus limit the attainment of all economic goals. All of these problems are widespread in the developing world in the 1970s. Concern about them often has dominated policy, with the result that less attention has been paid to long-run development.

4. A fourth pervasive concern among developing nations is to gain greater control over their own destiny and not be too subject to the decisions or preferences of foreigners. This concern is not surprising, given that many of the developing nations have emerged in the past quarter century from colonial status, in which their own interests were often quite secondary to those of the colonial powers. But the concern is not only about colonialism, the explicit form of which currently exists in only a few areas. The concern is about outside determination of a whole range of economic and political issues by the developed market economies, the centrally planned economies, or multinational corporations in what often is called "neocolonialism" or "neo-imperialism." Most developing countries do not want complete isolation or autarky. But they do want more control over their own destiny and a larger role in determining the nature of their international economic and political relations. This adds another important goal to our list—a goal that obviously is closely related to the overall subject of this book.

These and other concerns mean that it would be misleading to assume that the only economic aim of developing nations is to increase the growth rate of production or income per capita on a sustained basis. The earlier almost exclusive concentration on increasing average product per capita is too narrow for the last quarter of the twentieth century. As in other societies, there are a multiplicity of goals in the developing nations, some of which may be complementary and others of which may be conflicting. Nevertheless, the very low income levels experienced by hundreds of millions of people in the Third World means that increasing per capita income remains a major economic goal in most developing nations. Only by doing so will vast numbers of people be able to enjoy an existence that permits more than a constant struggle for bare survival. Only by doing so will such people be able to even partially develop their full human capabilities. However, efforts to increase per capita income will have to be accompanied by conscious policies directed toward the other concerns mentioned in this section if true development is to be attained.

1.2 THE DETERMINANTS OF ECONOMIC GROWTH AND DEVELOPMENT

Let us first focus on the determinants of the level of product or income, and therefore the change in product or income. Our considerations in this section are limited to internal ones. In the next section we consider how international trade modifies the situation.

What determines product or income levels? A simplified answer makes use of a production function, which is defined to give the maximum level of output of a good that can be produced for every combination of inputs (say human resources, natural resources, machinery and equipment, and so on). These maximum production levels obviously depend on the state of knowledge (or technology) and institutions and customs (for example, whether there typically are one, two, or three shifts of workers employed by firms).

For simplicity, suppose that an economy produces only two goods: agricultural products (A) and manufactured products (M). Assume also that at a point in time the economy has fixed supplies of all inputs and production relations that are given by the state of knowledge and the institutional framework. Then we can define the production possibility frontier for the economy as in Fig. 1.1.[4] On that frontier, all inputs are fully and efficiently employed. That is, the inputs are allocated between the two sectors so that there is no reallocation that would increase the output of one product without reducing the output of the other. If all inputs are fully and efficiently utilized in agriculture, A_5 units are produced. If all inputs are fully and efficiently utilized in manufacturing, M_5 units are produced. If both goods are produced and all inputs are fully and efficiently utilized, then production occurs at some intermediate point on the production possibility frontier, such as B with A_2 and M_2 units of the respective goods produced. If some of the inputs are used inefficiently or are unemployed, then production occurs inside the production possibility frontier (say at point C, with A_1 and M_1 units of the two goods).

If there is no international trade, the maximum production and income for the economy is given by the production possibility frontier. Because of inefficient utilization and unemployment of inputs, most economies in fact are at an interior point, such as C. Growth in product and income then depends on moving out toward the production possibility frontier and on

---

4 The production possibility frontier in Fig. 1.1 is drawn under the assumptions that there are not too great increasing returns to scale in either industry, that there is substitution possible among the basic inputs, and that agriculture and manufacturing would use different ratios of inputs if they faced the same input price ratios. For more details concerning the derivation of this frontier, see Appendix A or an intermediate microeconomics text.

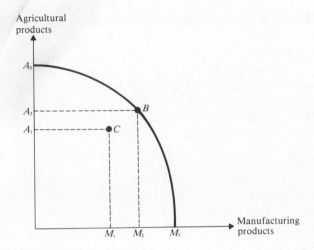

Fig. 1.1 Production possibility frontier

shifting the frontier outward. Movements toward the frontier occur with improvements in allocation and utilization of inputs, as induced perhaps by increases in total demand and/or by improvements in the functioning of markets or of planning boards. Outward movements of the production possibility frontier occur because of investment to increase the quantities of the basic inputs,[5] improvements in the state of knowledge that allow more output for a given input bundle, and output-increasing institutional change (such as changing from one shift of workers to two or three). The overall growth rate in production and in income is a weighted average of all of these changes. Because of an interest in what happens to individuals or families, however, focus usually is on the overall growth rate in production or income per capita.

That is the story in a nutshell. But what does it mean in more detail?

Historically it has meant that the greatest emphasis in thought on development and in development policy has been on increasing one input in the production process: the stocks of physical capital with which labor

---

5 Throughout this book the standard economics definition of investment is used: investment refers to the use of real resources to increase future consumption possibilities. Examples of investment include: building plants, machinery, and equipment; increasing inventories of raw materials, semi-processed or final goods; devoting resources to education or health or other forms of human capital. Note that this definition is not identical to the popular usage of the term of investment for the purchase of financial or other such assets, which may or may not be associated with the real investment referred to in the standard economic usage.

works. Classical economists, such as Adam Smith, emphasized the need for such capital accumulation to permit increased labor productivity through specialization.[6] Within his materialistic interpretation of history, Karl Marx argued that the accumulation of capital is the prime cause of development in industrialized societies. In the middle third of the twentieth century, this "capital fundamentalism" was quantified in the Harrod-Domar growth model, which in its simplest form states that the rate of growth of output is proportional to the savings rate out of income divided by the amount of additional capital that is required to generate one additional unit of output (or the incremental capital output ratio).[7]

What has this meant in terms of policy? Answers to this question have focused primarily on the need to increase savings, or the amount of current production that is not currently consumed but is instead used to expand the stock of physical capital. Internal tax, credit, and price policies have been directed toward shifting income toward groups that supposedly are high savers, such as the government and private industrialists.

A second related emphasis in policy has been to create more attractive private investment opportunities by government expenditures on social overhead capital such as transportation, communication, and irrigation systems. These policies may have aided somewhat in encouraging capital accumulation. But often they have also tended to increase inequalities in the distribution of income—frequently at the expense of the poorest members of society.

Although physical capital fundamentalism has dominated the analysis of development, there has long been some emphasis on the quality of the human input in the production process. In the early twentieth century, Joseph Schumpeter claimed that the critical factor in development was not adequate savings for physical capital investment, but the existence of entrepreneurs who would seize and develop investment opportunities.

More recently there has been substantial and growing emphasis on the need to improve the quality of the labor force through investment in "human capital" by education, health, sanitation, nutrition, and related programs. The returns on such investments in terms of increased product often have been quite high in comparison to those on physical capital investment. In addition to returns narrowly defined by increased measured

---

6 See Behrman [3] for a brief history of economic thought on the development process and for references to the leading contributions to that thought including those mentioned in this and the next section.

7 This relation is derived by asking what condition must be satisfied for an economy to be in Keynesian equilibrium over time. The answer in the simplest case is that the expansion in supply (related to the incremental capital output ratio) must just equal the expansion in demand (related to the marginal savings rate).

productivity, there may be considerable other benefits in terms of the welfare of the recipients. If such policies are directed toward the lower strata of society, moreover, they may lessen the inequality in the society and help raise some of the poorest out of extreme poverty. Quite often, however, the beneficiaries of these policies have not been concentrated in the poorest segment of society.

In addition to increasing the quantity and quality of inputs such as labor and physical capital, the production possibility frontier can be moved out by improvements in the state of knowledge and by institutional changes. A number of empirical studies conclude that the former is an important source of growth. However, the mechanism for inducing such technological change is not always so clear. Apparently it is associated with investment in physical and human capital, which reinforces the emphasis on those concerns. But attention also needs to be paid to the nature of the inducements for development of new technology, since often they are quite limited.

The ways in which institutional changes may move out the production possibility frontier or help in the attainment of other development goods are numerous. A few possible examples include the more intensive use of physical capital through the addition of more shifts of labor, changes in the ownership of assets through such acts as land reform, the integration of markets, the introduction of centralized or decentralized planning, the involvement of laborers in decision making by means of cooperatives or worker-managed establishments, the expansion of labor-intensive public works projects, the creation of more incentives for individual advancement, and the fuller incorporation of women into economic and related activities. These possibilities point to the fact that economic development involves not only economics narrowly defined, but also much subject matter from other academic fields such as political science, sociology, anthropology, psychology, and demography. Numerous controversies exist over the merits of many possible institutional changes. Unfortunately, the available empirical evidence in many cases is not very decisive in settling such controversies.

One example of such a controversy is the debate between advocates of planning and advocates of the free market to allocate resources in the developing countries. The latter group argues that too much information is required to plan successfully, markets are relatively efficient in allocating resources, people in developing countries—including poor peasants—are responsive to economic opportunities, and the use of markets economizes on some of the most scarce resources—decision-making capacities and information. To the extent that markets do not function well, the argument continues, they should be improved, not replaced.

Advocates of planning sometimes argue that markets might work all right for small changes but not for the necessary large changes. In the first two postwar decades a number of development economists perceived "vicious circles of poverty" or "low-level equilibrium traps" in which the results of poverty made it very difficult to escape from poverty. For example, low per capita income led to low savings that permitted little investment and therefore little expansion of the capacity to produce, and thus continued low per capita incomes. In order to break out of this state, what was required was a "critical minimum effort," a "big push," or a "take-off." Widespread coordination was needed to exploit the pecuniary external economics afforded by reduced intermediate input costs and increased demand in a "balanced growth" pattern. The government needed to invest in "social-overhead" capital such as transportation and communication systems in order to create the "preconditions" for the take-off, because the private sector would not invest sufficiently in such areas due to increasing returns to scale, technological externalities (that is, effects not captured by market prices), and public-good characteristics (that is, products such as improved weather forecasting, for which more use by one individual does not affect the possible use by others, so that markets do not allocate them efficiently). Planning could provide the necessary coordinated effort and motivational targets, assure consistency, use shadow prices that reflected the true scarcity value of resources, and incorporate social preferences and time rates of discount.[8]

1.3 FOREIGN TRADE IN THE ECONOMIC DEVELOPMENT PROCESS

Now let us consider how foreign trade enters into the economic development process. If there is international trade, national production is still limited by the production possibility frontier. However, in an important sense the country is no longer constrained to the inside or the boundary in respect to income and consumption decisions. Consider Fig. 1.2, in which the production possibility frontier is the same as in Fig. 1.1 but where the

---

8 Most individuals and societies do not value a good to be received in the future the same as they do one recieved in the present. Instead they discount the future good. Well-functioning markets incorporate the effect of individuals' discounting, but not necessarily the appropriate discounting by the collective of individuals that comprise a society. If the social and individual discount rates are identical, there is no problem. But the social discount rates may differ from individual rates. For example, all individuals may be willing to sacrifice more of current consumption for future generations if they knew every other individual was also sacrificing than they would if they thought it was an act in isolation. Such behavior implies a difference between social and individual discount rates that will not be reflected in well-functioning markets without policy interventions. Sections 5.2 gives an example of how discount rates can be used to compare incomes or expenditures at different points time.

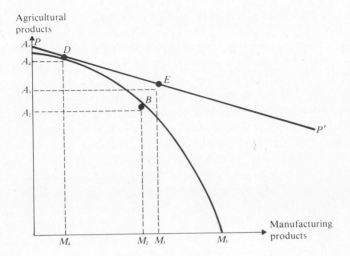

Figure 1.2

developing country of interest is assumed to be able to trade on the international market. Assume that the country is too small to affect international prices, but can trade as much as it wants at the international price ratio of M to A, which is indicated be the slope of the straight line PP'.[9] Further, suppose that there is no problem of inefficient usage or of unemployment of inputs, so that production is on the production possibility frontier. Without international trade, the country can choose any point on the frontier for its production and use. Suppose that it selects point B, with A_2 units of agricultural goods and M_2 units of manufactured goods. With the possibility of international trade, however, the country can generally do better. Given the PP' international price line, for example, it could produce A_4 and M_4 at D, trade $A_4 - A_3$ for $M_3 - M_4$ to move to E, and there have both more agricultural and more manufactured goods to use than it would have with no trade at point B! Therefore, specialization in production of the good(s) in which

9 The line PP' gives the terms on which the country can trade on the international market. If it exchanges A for M to go from point D to point E, for example, it must give up $P_A (A_4 - A_3)$ dollars worth of A in order to get $P_M(M_3 - M_4)$ dollars worth of M. These two dollar values must be equal if the country is in equilibrium in regard to its balance of payments with the rest of the world. The expression equating them may be solved to obtain the price ratio of manufactured to agricultural goods in the international market: $P_M/P_A = (A_4 - A_3)/(M_3 - M_4)$, which is the slope of the PP' line. To assume that the country cannot affect international prices by the amount it trades is to assume that this price ratio is .constant and therefore that the international price line is straight.

the economy has a comparative advantage and trading for the other good(s) on the international market provide another means by which a country may increase the per capita availability of goods for the use of its citizens.

But surely this situation could not be realistic! If this developing country is gaining from international trade, are not its trading partners losing? And if they are losing, will they not refuse to trade?

David Ricardo answered these questions in 1817 with his systemization of the gains from international trade. In his theory of comparative advantage he demonstrated that all countries could gain if each specialized in the production of the commodity for which it had a comparative advantage.

Figure 1.3 provides a simple two-country illustration of the theory of comparative advantage. For simplicity, assume that production requires only one input,[10] labor, of which both countries have two hundred hours per day. Further assume that in the developed country one hour of labor is required to produce one unit of agricultural products (A), and one half-hour of labor is required to produce one unit of manufacturing goods (M). Also assume that the developing nation is less efficient in producing both goods, requiring two hours of labor to produce either one unit of A or one unit of M. If there is no international trade, each country is limited in the choices indicated by its respective production possibility frontier (the solid lines in Fig. 1.3).

Now suppose that the possibility of international trade is allowed and the equilibrium ratio of international prices of agricultural to manufactured goods is 3 to 2 (as given by the dashed lines in Fig. 1.3).[11] Now the developed country can specialize in M and trade along the international price line that is above its production possibility curve everywhere.[12] The developing country can also specialize in A and trade along the international price line that is above its production possibility curve. Even though the developing

---

10 This assumption, together with the assumed constant labor-output coefficients independent of the scale of production (that is, constant returns to scale), ensures that in this simple example the production possibility frontiers are straight lines instead of being curved as in Figs. 1.1 and 1.2. Because of this assumption, both countries specialize completely in the production of one good. With curved production possibility frontiers, less than complete specialization probably would occur.

11 Without the underlying supply and demand curves, we cannot determine the equilibrium price ratio. However, it is in between the no-trade ratios implied by the labor requirements of two in the developed country and of one in the developing country. For this example we are simply assuming a value half-way in between.

12 The only exception is where the international price line and the production possibility frontier intersect on the M axis. At this point the developed country produces and uses 400 units of M and 0 units of A and does not trade internationally. A similar observation holds for the developing country at 100 units of A and 0 units of M.

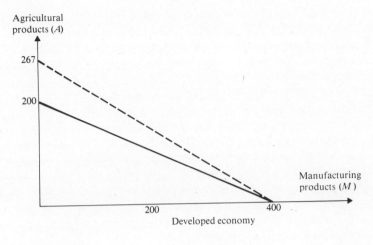

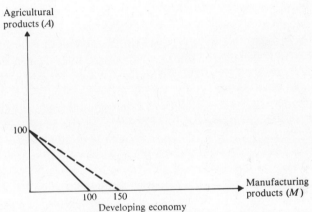

Fig. 1.3 Illustration of comparative advantage

country is less efficient in producing both *A* and *M*, *both* countries are better off if each specializes in the production of the good in which it has a *relative* or *comparative* advantage and they trade. The returns to inputs (in this case, the wages of laborers) rise in both countries. The Ricardian comparative advantage theory is indeed a powerful argument for international trade!

Moreover, international trade offers other advantages to the developing country. Critical inputs for which there is not a good domestic supply— such as petroleum for the non-oil-producing countries—can be imported. The same is often true for physical capital goods, since many of the developing economies are not large enough to support an efficient machine tool industry. Moreover, such capital inputs can facilitate the importation of technical knowledge, which pushes out the production possibility frontier. Finally, the existence of foreign competition can induce greater efficiency in domestic production and lessen the development of local monopolies.

But there are some reservations—which some argue are more than off-setting. These have to do with the varying of the international price ratio, the attainment of goals other than that of increasing per capita income, or dynamic developments over time.

Consider first the possibility of varying the international price ratio. Some developing countries produce a large share of the world production of a given commodity and thus may be able to affect its price. Examples include Ghana with cocoa and Brazil with coffee. Alternatively, a group of producing countries acting together may be able to affect the price of their exports.[13] In such a case the international price ratio line in Figs. 1.2 and 1.3 is no longer straight but bends downwards, since the more units of A that are exported the less is the price received.

The second possibility is that other goals are more important than the attainment of the level of consumption possible with free trade—and these goals cannot be otherwise attained more easily. For example, a goal may be to transfer resources from the producers of exports to the producers of industrial goods. If direct transfers cannot be made by income taxes and subsidies, the goal might be best pursued by interfering with international trade (for example, taxing exports and using protective tariffs for industrial imports). Yet another example would be the desire to have greater control over the destiny of the country than might occur with free trade.

The third possibility is related to the dynamics of comparative advantage over time. Certain aspects of this possibility were recognized by the classical economists by the mid-nineteenth century, but in the immediate postwar period the most articulate proponent was Raúl Prebisch and the Economic Commission for Latin America (ECLA). There is both a shorter-run and a longer-run component to this view.

The shorter-run component is that fluctuations in the international markets cause particularly large instabilities in the export revenues of the developing countries.[14] Such fluctuations are costly because they make long-run resource allocation decisions difficult and because they cause short-run instabilities in employment and in prices in the developing countries. Therefore, some interference with free international trade may be desirable.

The longer-run component is that immediate (or static) comparative advantage may not reflect long-run (or dynamic) comparative advantage. But

---

13 4.3 below reviews such historical efforts.

14 Section 4.1 below considers the historical evidence about the degree of such fluctuations.

exploiting fully the immediate comparative advantage may make it impossible to benefit fully from the long-run comparative advantage. This is so for two reasons: (1) Capital inputs cannot be shifted easily from the sector in which there is an immediate advantage to the one in which there is the long-run advantage. (2) The long-run advantage can be realized only by developing necessary skills through expanding production in the relevant sector now, even though immediate comparative advantage would argue against such an expansion. Moreover, the argument continues, international price levels tend to turn against the primary (that is, agricultural and mineral) commodities that the developing countries tend to export and in favor of the manufactured goods they tend to import.[15] This occurs because of the lower responsiveness in demand to increasing income for primary products as opposed to manufactured ones and because of the concentration of market power in the industrialized nations. Therefore, the developing countries should realize that their long-run or dynamic comparative advantage is more in the production of manufactured goods than the immediate situation indicates, so they should interfere with free trade to encourage greater industrialization.

In response to such reservations, the theory of comparative advantage for the developing countries must be modified. Except in extreme cases in which isolation is an important goal in itself, however, the arguments for comparative advantage are only modified, not rejected. In general, developing countries can gain by consuming outside of the production possibility frontier through international trade. This still leaves open the question of whether or not such gains are used in part to alleviate the mass poverty emphasized above. But the expansion of command over resources that results from international trade at least increases the options of dealing with the mass poverty problem.

1.4 CONCLUSIONS

In my judgment, the most important economic problem of the last quarter of the twentieth century is how to alleviate the mass poverty afflicting hundreds of millions of persons in the developing world. The extent to which there will be success in this venture will depend primarily on the internal transformation of the developing economies. We have explored briefly some of the relevant interval aspects of the development process.

But the nature of the international environment in which the developing nations operate also can make a difference. And it is this interface between the developing and developed nations that is affected most directly by the policies of the United States and of other developed nations. The develop-

---

15 Section 4.2 below examines the recent historical evidence relevant to this claim.

ing nations have called for a new international economic order, with international commodity agreements for their major exports at the heart of this call. This call raises a number of important questions: What would be the impact of such agreements on the consumers of coffee, copper, and the other relevant commodities? What would be the costs? Would such arrangements be viable? And, probably most important in my view, would they significantly increase the capability of the developing nations to alleviate the overwhelming problems of mass poverty? This book tries to explore such critical questions.

REFERENCES

1. The World Bank Group. *World Bank Atlas, 1975: Population, Per Capita Product, and Growth Rates.* Washington, D.C.: World Bank, 1975.

2. E. F. Schumacher. *Small is Beautiful: Economics as if People Mattered.* New York: Harper & Row, 1973.

3. J. r. Behrman. *"Development Economics" in Modern Economic Thought.* Ed. by S. Weintraub. Philadelphia: University of Pennsylvania Press, 1977.

Recent Experience of the Developing Countries and the call for a New International Economic Order

2

To provide further perspective about the development process and the call for a new international economic order, Section 2.1 reviews the recent experience of the developing nations. Particular emphasis is placed on foreign-sector considerations. Then Section 2.2 presents a brief summary of the call for a new international economic order, the analysis of the most important components of which is the subject of the rest of this book. Section 2.3 provides a conclusion.

2.1 RECENT DEVELOPMENT EXPERIENCE

The 1960s were declared to be the First Development Decade by the United Nations. A major target was a growth rate in the real national product[1] of the developing nations of 5.0 percent. This target was considered by many to be ambitious at the time of its adoption. The 1970s were designated the Second Development Decade, with generally somewhat higher targets.

Since the commencement of the First Development Decade, the developing nations have made major progress in their development. Taken as a group, they have achieved most of the overall targets for accelerated development adopted by the United Nations. Their rate of progress has been far greater than that of the developed market economies at a comparable stage of development. During the First Development Decade their real national product grew at an average annual rate of 5.5 percent, significantly

---

1 Real national product means the economic product of a nation after adjusting for price changes.

exceeding the target noted above.[2] During the first half of the Second Development Decade, there was further acceleration, with a growth rate approaching the target of 6.0 percent (although there was some slowdown in the mid 1970s). The rate of growth in real industrial production approximated the target of 8.0 percent, and the overall ratio of savings to national product exceeded 20 percent, well above the United Nations' target.

In substantial part, the economic growth of developing countries in the 1960s and early 1970s was export-led, in response to growing world markets. The rapid growth in the developed market economies provided expanding trade outlets and a powerful external stimulus to many developing economies. The centrally planned economies also significantly increased their purchases in international markets. As a result, major increases were experienced in prices and trade volumes of primary commodities that the developing nations export, such as petroleum, coffee, and copper. Export earnings from manufacturing were a smaller proportion of the total, but grew even more rapidly. Section 1.3 discusses how these expanded earnings from trade, supplemented by net financial inflows, facilitate the attainment of economic goals of the developing countries.

Despite apparent success by several aggregate indicators, a number of observers have expressed increasing dissatisfaction with what has been happening. Among their reasons are the following.

First, even if the developing countries grow faster than the developed market economies, they are not likely to grow sufficiently faster to keep the gap in per capita incomes from increasing for some time. For example, suppose that real per capita income grew at 1 percent per year in the developed market economies and twice as fast in the developing countries. Given the current differences noted in Section 1.1 in average per capita incomes between the two groups, it would be over 180 years before the gap in per capita incomes between the two country groups began to narrow. If real per capita income grew at 2.0 percent in the developed market economies and at 4.0 percent in the developing countries, it would require almost a century for the gap to begin to narrow. Thus, even under the assumption that the developing countries grew much faster than the developed ones, the real income gap will be increasing for decades, if not centuries. And it does not seem likely that real per capita income in the developing countries will grow twice as fast as in the developed nations for any sustained period. Therefore, as measured by the income gap, the developing countries are likely to fall further behind for some time.

2 The difference between annual growth rates of 5.0 and 5.5 percent may not seem like much. But the two rates result in much different outcomes if maintained over a long period due to what has been referred to as the "magic of compound interest." For example, over a century the 5.5 percent annual growth rate results in a level of product or income over 60 percent higher than does the 5.0 percent annual growth rate.

Second, the relative success at the aggregate level obscures a wide range of experiences on the national level. Some developing countries have been doing quite well in the development decades. Examples include Brazil, Taiwan, Barbados, Cyprus, Republic of Korea, Hong Kong, Singapore, Swaziland, and the smaller OPEC (Organization of Petroleum Exporting Countries) oil-rich nations. However, many other countries have been doing quite poorly. And the latter group includes many of the poorest countries, especially in South Asia and sub-Saharan Africa. Therefore, per capita income disparities have been growing among the developing countries. Moreover, recent growth in agricultural production in the developing countries has been at only about half of the Second Development Decade target rate of 4 percent per year. In the face of rapid population growth, per capita food production actually has declined. Partially because of the relative stagnation in agriculture, income distribution often worsened within many countries, as well as among countries.

Third, short-run stability problems have intensified in many cases. Unemployment increased in many countries, in part because of limited agricultural growth. Worldwide inflationary pressures exacerbated many inflationary problems originating partially internally. Among the oil-importing nations especially, import costs soared after the OPEC petroleum price increases of 400 percent in 1973-1974. Grain importers also faced very large price increases at about the same time. The results included very large balance-of-foreign-payments deficits, curtailed imports, large accumulated foreign debt obligations, and abandonment or suspension of many development programs.

Fourth, the non-oil-exporting developing countries continued to perceive that their economies were strongly subjected to external forces over which they had little control. Multinational corporations operated with little apparent heed to the aspirations of host developing countries. International organizations, such as the General Agreement on Trade and Tariffs (GATT) and the International Monetary Fund (IMF), were dominated by the developed market economies and operated primarily in the interests of such economies. International primary commodities markets on which the developing countries were so dependent for critical foreign exchange were characterized by considerable fluctuations and downward secular trends in prices relative to the prices of imports.[3]

2.2 THE CALL FOR A NEW INTERNATIONAL ECONOMIC ORDER

In the years immediately following the Second World War, international interactions were heavily conditioned by the bipolarism of the Cold War. The developing countries attempted to establish another group that repre-

---

3 See Chapter 4.

sented the interests of neither of the blocks in the Cold War, but instead the interests of the Third World. In the late 1950s and early 1960s some progress was made toward this end by the creation of a nonaligned country group. The first Summit Conference of Non-Aligned Countries met in Belgrade in 1961 under the initiative of the heads of state of Egypt (Nasser), India (Nehru), and Yugoslavia (Tito). At about the same time the developing countries succeeded in creating more emphasis in international forums on their problems by having the United Nations declare the 1960s to be the First Development Decade.

Shortly thereafter, further success was attained within the United Nations by the creation of UNCTAD (United Nations Conference on Trade and Development), an organization with an explicit mandate to focus on the problems of the developing world. In 1964, UNCTAD I, the first meeting of this new organization, was held in Geneva, Switzerland. UNCTAD I sought methods to expand world trade, spur economic development, and increase the incomes of the Third World. It placed considerable emphasis on comprehensive international commodity agreements (that is, agreements including provisions not only for prices and quantities, but also for coordination of national production and consumption policies, for guaranteed acces to markets, and for limiting the expansion of synthetic competitors) in order "to raise progressively the amount of foreign exchange at the disposal of the developing countries." Also at UNCTAD I, the Group of 77 was formed by the representatives of the seventy-seven developing nations at the Geneva sessions. The Group of 77 evolved to represent the Third World interests at the United Nations and other international forums.

Four years later, UNCTAD II was held in New Dehli, India. Priority was given to discussions of generalized trading preferences, by which the developed market economies would grant preferential international trading arrangements to the manufactured and processed products of the developing world. The goals and principles concerning international commodity agreements of UNCTAD I were reendorsed and permanent committees were established on commodities and on synthetics and substitutes. At UNCTAD III, in Santiago, Chile in 1972, the necessity for commodity pricing policies relevant to the needs of the developing countries continued to be stressed, and twenty-seven commodities were identified as needing further international consultation. There also was greater emphasis than at UNCTAD I and II on trade liberalization and expansion of exports, which facilitated greater agreement with the major importers.

Despite the establishment of UNCTAD, the Group of 77, and other international organizations favorable to or dominated by the developing countries, in the early 1970s frustrations increased in the Third World about the development process, international economic relations, and the limited control of the developing nations over their own destiny. As is noted at the end of the previous section, this frustration intensified in spite of the apparent aggregate success of the developing world in meeting the fairly ambitious targets of the development decades.

In late 1973, the Arab petroleum exporters agreed to an oil embargo to attempt to force change in the Middle Eastern policies of the developed market nations. In December of 1973, they joined the other OPEC nations in doubling the price of oil, beginning a process that quadrupled the price in about a year. Since most of the developing nations depend on imported petroleum for basic energy and on important petroleum-based products, such as fertilizer, most of the developing world (as well as many of the developed countries) were affected very negatively by the OPEC policies. Deficits in international payments soared, imports were curtailed, foreign debts multiplied, and development plans were suspended because of these problems. It seemed possible that the somewhat fragile alliance among the Third World countries would be torn asunder by the OPEC actions. Some observers thought that the oil-importing developing countries would find it in their own best self-interests to join the developed market economies in a concentrated effort to break the OPEC cartel.

However, that did not occur. Instead, President Boumediènne of Algeria took the initiative in calling the Sixth Special Session of the General Assembly of the United Nations on Raw Materials and Development in April and May of 1974. At this conference it was argued that the current economic problems of the non-OPEC developing nations arose *not* from the recent petroleum price increases, but from a faulty international economic system that had persistently neglected their economic development needs in general and that had underpaid them for their commodity exports (including oil) in particular. The non-OPEC developing countries were asked to accept higher petroleum prices as the vanguard of a new international economic order that also would seek to improve substantially the terms of international trade for the other primary products on which the Third World depends for the majority of its export revenues. It was a bold stroke in support of generally higher international primary prices and of new producer associations modeled after OPEC.

The OPEC strategy succeeded in getting the support of the other Third World countries. Past UNCTAD proposals for improving the international economic opportunities of the developing countries were integrated in this spirit into a "Declaration on the Establishment of a New International Economic Order" and a "Programme of Action." [4] These documents were adopted by acclamation, but some of the developed countries clearly were less than enthusiastic. The proposals were of varying specificity, import-

---

4 These and a number of related documents are reproduced in Erb and Kallab [1].

ance, and controversy. A number already had been or soon were accepted, at least in principle. Examples include the progressive removal of trade barriers, liberalization of compensatory financing schemes that provide funds from the IMF (International Monetary Fund) for short-run shortfalls in the value of exports, and generalized trade preferences in favor of the exports of the developing countries. Others have been much more controversial—especially the proposals for lessening the fluctuations and increasing the trend of real prices of commodity exports of the developing countries, which are central to the overall call and the subject of primary interest in this book. Considerable confrontation developed between the developing and developed nations over these and other issues.

Beyond the specific proposals, also of substantial importance in the Declaration and Programme for a New International Economic Order is the stated interest of developing countries in having a much larger role in working out their aspirations for developmental progress through greater and more stable access to the markets of the developed countries. They forcibly raised the issue of better integration of their international trade and investment in the global pattern of international relations that has evolved primarily among industrial countries. They showed determination to have a say in changing the international system so that it is more responsive to their needs and interests.

Subsequent international meetings of the developing countries emphasized the centrality in their case for a new international economic order of problems relating to fluctuations and secular trends in the prices of their commodity exports. These emphases are reflected in the Declaration and Action Programme of the Conference of Developing Countries on Raw Materials adopted in Dakar, Senegal in February 1975 and at the 20th Conference of Commonwealth Heads of State or Government at Kingston, Jamaica in April 1975. At the same time the confrontation between the developing and developed nations, or the South and the North, seemed to intensify. Indicative of this problem was the closing in April 1975 of the Preliminary Working Sessions for the Conference on International Economic Cooperation (CIEC) without the tripartite representatives (from the developed, non-oil-developing, and oil nations) even being able to agree on a future agenda.

In September 1975 the tendency for increasing North-South conflict over international economic relations was reversed at least temporarily at the Seventh Special Session of the United Nations General Assembly on Development and International Economic Cooperation. Of key importance in this change was the cooperative attitude displayed by the United States through its Secretary of State, Henry Kissinger. It is hoped that a new era of serious bargaining to replace previous confrontations was begun. A General Assembly resolution instructed UNCTAD IV (to be held in Nairobi, Kenya in May 1976) that "an important aim . . . should be to reach decisions on the improvement of market structures in the field of raw materials and commodities of export interest to the developing countries, including decisions with respect to an integrated programme and the applicability of elements thereof.'' UNCTAD increased its already considerable activities in this area.

In February 1976 the Group of 77 (which by then included 112 developing countries) drew up the so-called Manila Declaration in preparation for UNCTAD IV. This declaration consists of seventeen major economic reforms, together with what Lewis [2] characterizes as ''a threatening pledge, 'to make full use of the bargaining power of the developing countries through joint and united action' to secure these aims.'' The centerpiece of the declaration is support for the UNCTAD promoted proposal of an integrated commodity program financed by a common fund.

With this backing the UNCTAD [3] secretariat prepared its final proposal for the UNCTAD IV Nairobi meetings. The broad objectives of this proposal are:

(i) to improve the terms of trade of developing countries, and to ensure an adequate rate of growth in the purchasing power of their aggregate earnings from their exports of primary commodities, while minimizing short-term fluctuations in those earnings; and

(ii) to encourage more orderly development of world commodity markets in the interests of both producers and consumers.

The proposal recommends focus on seventeen commodities, which cover about three-quarters of the non-petroleum commodity trade of the developing countries. These include ten ''core'' commodities (cocoa, coffee, copper, sugar, cotton, jute, rubber, sisal, tea, and tin) and seven others (bananas, bauxite, beef and veal, iron ore, rice, wheat, and wool). The ten ''core'' commodities account for about three-quarters of the export value of developing countries of all seventeen commodities, are relatively storable, and are recommended for initial individual international stockpiling agreements.

To ensure adequate financing for these agreements, the proposal advocates the establishment of a $6 billion common fund by subscriptions from importers and exporters of these commodities (with exceptions for the poorest nations). This fund would serve a catalytic role in stimulating new commodity stockpile arrangements by ensuring adequate finances independent of the particular financial difficulties of the individual countries participating in a specific commodity agreement. The common fund also would pool and reduce risks[5] and have more bargaining power in international

---

5 The reduction of risks through pooling or diversifying is an important principle underlying the operation of insurance companies.

capital markets than could a set of individual funds for the same commodities. It also would require smaller financing than the aggregate of a set of individual funds because of differences in the phasing of cycles across commodity markets.

The developed countries also approached UNCTAD IV with increased interest in international primary commodity agreements. The 400-percent rise in OPEC oil prices in late 1973 and early 1974 and the general increase in commodity prices in 1971-1974[6] aided in the creation of a "scarcity mentality" and acute concern over the "access to supplies." In the United States the Trade Act of 1974 directed the President to negotiate access to supply agreements, and the National Commission on Supplies and Shortages, was instructed to report to the President and to Congress on the causes of the 1973-1974 material shortages and on proposals to lessen the possibility of repetition of that experience through economic stockpiles, better information systems, and other means. The executive director of this commission, George Eads [5], reported that the discussions of the commission with private companies "tell of a new concern on their part for stability and continuity of supply—even if it means that they must pay higher prices." Because of the much greater dependence on imported commodities, in much of Europe the concerns about access to supply were greater than in the United States.

Although both the developing and developed country groups expressed strong interest in integrated commodity agreements, there remained significant differences. The developing countries, for example, emphasized the assurance of a "just" return to producers and indexation of commodity prices by tying them to movements in the price index of their imports. The United States, as represented by Secretary of State Kissinger [6], focused more on the need for expanded resource supplies through the establishment of an International Resource Bank, ensuring access to supply, stabilization (in part through compensatory finance), and, in the words of Deputy Assistant Secretary for Economic and Business Affairs Katz [7], "seeking an open world economy that permits market forces to operate with minimum restrictions on the flow of goods, services, capital, and technology across international boundaries."

UNCTAD IV entailed a month of tense negotiations. At times the shift from confrontation to cooperation that had occurred at the Seventh Special Session of the General Assembly the previous September seemed about to

---

6 Cooper and Lawrence [4] report that in the 115 years for which the *Economist* price index for all non-fuel commodities is available, in no one previous year was the increase as great as the 63 percent experienced in 1972-1973 and in no previous three-year period was it as large as the 159 percent experienced in 1971-1974.

be reversed. At the end, at least superficial conciliation prevailed.[7] The conference adopted a resolution for an "Integrated Programme for Commodities." This resolution has an introduction and three substantive parts:[8] (1) Objectives, (2) Commodity Coverage, and (3) International Measures of the Programme. It is useful to describe each of these in some detail since this resolution has set the framework for subsequent discussions on international commodity agreements.

The two major immediate *objectives* are: (1) the stabilization of the relevant international commodity markets, and (2) the improvement in the real income that developing countries receive from commodity exports. Stabilization apparently refers primarily to the "avoidance of excessive price fluctuations," although lessening fluctuations in earnings is also mentioned. (As is discussed in Section 3.1, these two ends are not necessarily compatible). In statements concerning the improvement of real income of the developing country exporters, reference is made to "renumerative and just" prices for producers that "take account of world inflation" and stabilization "around a growing trend" of export earnings. Even though these phrases readily permit an interpretation that something akin to indexation (tying the prices of the exports of interest to movements in some price index, such as that for the imports of the developing countries) is implied,[9] no explicit use of that term occurs because it had become a politically unacceptable symbol to some of the leading developed nations.

Other objectives relate to access to demand and to supply, "equitable" prices to consumers, the promotion of equilibrium between supply and demand, diversification of production of the developing countries, improving market structure, increasing the participation of developing countries in distribution and transport of the commodities, and increasing the competitiveness of natural products relative to synthetics through research and development. Some of these are compatible with the two major objectives, others are potentially conflicting (for example, the interest of producers

---

7 Lewis [2], however, characterizes the developed countries as being "sharply divided over the wisdom of this approach." He notes that the United Kingdom and the Federal Republic of Germany expressed "reservations" about the resolution, and that the United States insisted that the preparatory talks be held "without commitment" and that the passage of the resolution did not change its "known views on the new international economic order," but that a group of sixteen other industrial countries gave broad support to the resolution.

8 There also is a Part 4 entitled "Procedures and Time-Table."

9 On the other hand statements about "equitable" prices to consumers and promoting "equilibrium between supply and demand within expanding world commodity trade" at a minimum create ambiguity about such an interpretation.

versus consumers),[10] and others are so general that the specific implications are quite unclear.

The *commodity coverage* starts with the ten "core" commodities indicated above, although they are not singled out explicitly in this manner. The above list of other commodities is supplemented by adding manganese, phosphates, tropical timber, and vegetable oils. Also beef and veal, rice, wheat, and wool are not included explicitly, although it is recognized that changes may occur once negotiations are under way. The basic focus thus remains the same as in the UNCTAD [3] proposal, with some modifications to exclude the basic grains that are to be covered elsewhere and to weight the composition somewhat more toward the developing countries.

The *international measures of the programme* focus on the establishment of international commodity stockpiling arrangements to keep prices within negotiated ranges "which could be periodically reviewed and appropriately revised, taking into account, *inter alia,* movements in prices of imported manufactured goods, exchange rates, production costs and world inflation, and levels of production and consumption." The international stockpiles will be coordinated with national stockpiles, supply management measures for production and exports, and, when appropriate, multilateral long-term supply and purchase commitments. Efforts will be made to improve information about market conditions. Negotiations will be initiated for a common fund to facilitate the establishment of such agreements. Special measures will be adopted to protect the interests of the least developed countries.

Other measures include improvement and enlargement of compensatory financing of export earnings of developing countries "around a growing trend"; improvement of market access for primary and processed commodities of developing nations through multilateral trade negotiations and generalized preferences; improvement of the capacity of developing countries to participate in the processing, transportation, distribution, and marketing of commodities; the encouragement of research and development to improve the competitiveness of natural products with synthetics and consideration of the harmonization of natural and synthetic supplies; and consideration of special measures for commodities "whose problems cannot be adequately solved by stocking and which experience a persistent price decline."

The specificity and political practicality of these proposals vary enormously. It is quite clear what a further expansion of the IMF compensatory primary facility might mean in terms of increasing the funding available to developing countries that experience a decline in their export earnings, for example. But the explicit steps for harmonization with synthetic supplies or

---

10 See also the previous note.

for the nonstorable products are much more vague. How these measures relate to some of the objectives, such as "equitable" prices for consumers and diversification of production in developing nations, also is not very clear.

After UNCTAD IV, strong arguments continued to be presented for and against the institution of international commodity arrangements. In the first half of 1977 in Paris the tripartite representatives (from the developed, non-oil-developing, and oil nations) at the Conference on International Economic Cooperation (CIEC) endorsed the further exploration and development of international commodity agreements under the aegis of UNCTAD. While the exact details of the UNCTAD IV resolution may not be implemented, it is clear that this resolution has established the framework for debate over these important issues during the late 1970s and early 1980s.

2.3 CONCLUSIONS

On an aggregate level the economic performance of the developing countries has been faily good in the past decade and a half, at least in comparison to the experience of the developed economies at a similar stage. Nevertheless, considerable dissatisfaction has been widespread and growing in the developing countries. The sources of this dissatisfaction include the perceptions that the gap between the developing and developed economies will continue to grow for some time, that some of the poorest among the developing countries have been faring relatively poorly, that short-run problems for the developing economies intensified in the 1970s, and that the developing countries have had little impact on the international economic environment in which they operate. UNCTAD and other international organizations have provided forums for expressing this dissatisfaction and for promoting proposals for improving the lot of the developing countries. Until the early 1970s, however, such discussions were mostly fragmented and rhetorical.

The success of the oil-producing countries of OPEC in increasing petroleum prices substantially starting in 1973 served as a catalyst to pull together the developing countries in support of a call for a New International Economic Order in which the interests of the developing countries would be represented better. This call integrated many of the proposals that had been discussed previously at UNCTAD and elsewhere. At the heart of the call is the proposal for international commodity agreements. This proposal was formalized in the resolution in favor of an integrated commodity program at UNCTAD IV, in Nairobi in 1976. The resolution places primary immediate emphasis on two objectives for ten core commodity markets: (1) stabilization and (2) improvement in the real income that developing countries receive from commodity exports. Subsequent international meetings have reaffirmed the exploration and development of international commodity agreements under the aegis of UNCTAD.

Whether or not the exact details of the UNCTAD resolution on international commodity agreements are implemented, it is clear that this resolution has established a basic reference point for debate on these issues in the late 1970s and early 1980s. The outcome of this debate may have great importance for the developing countries and for the consumers of coffee, copper, and the other commodities that are involved. But there remains considerable dispute about what would happen if the UNCTAD resolution or some related international commodity agreements were implemented. This book attempts to clarify the issues by an investigation of the impact of international commodity agreements through three modes of analysis: (1) an examination of some important theoretical questions; (2) an examination of the historical experience of commodity price movements and of international commodity agreements; and (3) simulations of the proposed international commodity programs. Each of these approaches is considered, in turn, in the chapters that follow.

REFERENCES

1. G. F. Erb and V. Kallab (Eds). *Beyond Dependency: The Developing World Speaks Out*. Washington, D.C.: Overseas Development Council, 1975.

2. P. Lewis. "The Have-Nots are Gaining Ground in Their Drive to Gain Concessions." *National Journal*, 774-82 (5 June 1976).

3. UNCTAD. "An Integrated Commodity Programme." Geneva: UNCTAD, 1976.

4. R. N. Cooper and R. Z. Lawrence. "The 1972-1975 Commodity Boom." *Brookings Papers on Economic Activity* 3: 671-715 (1975).

5. G. C. Eads. "Address of Executive Director of National Commission on Supplies and Shortages before the Section of Natural Resources Law, American Bar Association Convention, Atlanta, Georgia, August 10, 1976."

6. H. A. Kissinger. "UNCTAD IV: Expanding Cooperation for Global Economic Development." Speech of 6 May 1976 before the Fourth Ministerial Meeting of UNCTAD in Nairobi.

7. J. L. Katz. "International Commodity Policy." Statement by Deputy Assistant Secretary for Economic and Business Affairs before the House Subcommittee on International Organizations; International Policy; and International Trade and Commerce (1976).

Simple Theoretical 3
Analysis of
International
Commodity
Agreements

Simple economic theory provides useful guidelines for considering some important issues about which there is some confusion in much of the speculation about commodity market agreements. Therefore it is useful to discuss briefly the following four theoretical questions: What are the implications of price stabilization attempts for producers' revenues? Who benefits from stabilization? What are the normative implications of market solutions to economic problems? Under what conditions is it probable that collusive action by producers alone can raise market prices? Each of the first four sections in this chapter explores one of these questions. The last section gives conclusions.

3.1 IMPLICATIONS OF PRICE STABILIZATION ATTEMPTS FOR VARIABILITY AND LEVEL OF PRODUCERS' REVENUES

Advocates of international commodity agreements recognize that stabilization of export revenues probably is of much more interest to the developing countries than is stabilization of prices. In principle, of course, a buffer stock authority might buy and sell with the intent of stabilizing revenues.[1] Such an operation would be much more difficult than price stabilization,

---

1 It could attempt to act so that the total market demand curve facing producers approached a unit elastic curve with constant revenue implications. Elasticity is defined below as the percentage change in quantity in response to a given percentage change in price. For a unit elastic demand curve this value is unitary or one. Therefore as one moves along the demand curve every change of x percent in price causes a change of x percent in the opposite direction of the quantity demand, so revenue (the product of the two) remains constant.

however, for several reasons. Day-to-day operations would be harder because of the greater lags in the availability of quantity than price data. If such an arrangement were successful, strong inducements would exist for supply reductions because the same revenues could be earned with lower sales, which would release factors of production for other uses.[2] The concurrence of importing nations with a revenue-stabilizing scheme, finally, seems unlikely.

For such reasons, advocates of international commodity agreements argue for price stabilization instead of revenue stabilization. But this strategy raises the question: What are the implications of price stabilization attempts for revenues?

A preeminent international economist, Harry G. Johnson [1], states that "elementary economic analysis" suggests that international commodity agreements are dubious on these grounds. His argument is illustrated in Fig. 3.1. The basic average supply and demand curves for a purely competitive international commodity market are given by solid straight lines. The average supply curve (SS) gives the average quantity supplied for each possible price.[3] The average demand curve (DD) gives the average quantity demanded for each possible price. The assumption of pure competition implies that the total market supply is the sum of the quantities supplied at various prices by a large number of individual producers, each of whose production is so small that it cannot perceptibly change the market price by altering its quantity supplied. There is a parallel assumption on the demand side. The solid supply curve is an average curve in the sense that it is halfway between the two equally likely dashed-line actual supply curves, where the different locations reflect differences in some nonprice supply determinant (say, good and bad weather). A parallel situation holds for demand due to two different and equally likely values of some determinant of demand other than price (say, high and low income). P_0 is the average equilibrium price, at which level average quantity demanded just equals average quantity supplied (and both equal Q_0). P_0 also is the price at which the buffer stock is assumed to stabilize prices by purchasing the commodity if otherwise the price would fall, and selling it if otherwise the price would rise.

---

2 Such an outcome probably would not occur if there were a large number of relatively small producers each operating independently, but only if supply were organized in decision units of large enough size so that their individual impact on market prices was noticeable.

3 In Fig. 3.1a, for example, only the demand curve shifts so that the supply curve is traced out. When the demand curve is high the equilibrium price is P_2 and the quantity supplied is Q_2. When the demand curve is low the equilibrium price is P_1 and the quantity supplied is Q_1. The loci of quantities supplied at different prices (such as Q_2 at P_2 and Q_1 at P_1) is the supply curve.

Similar comments apply for the demand curve in Fig. 3.1b.

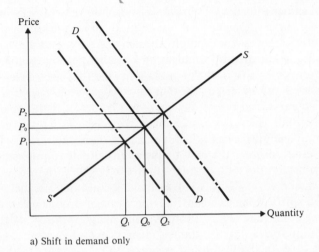

a) Shift in demand only

Fig. 3.1 Impact on revenues of shifts in demand and supply curves with and without price stabilization at P_0 by a buffer stock

Consider first the case of instability due to demand shifts alone (Fig. 3.1a). Without price stabilization, producers' revenues are $P_2 * Q_2$ when the demand curve is shifted up and $P_1 * Q_1$ when the demand curve is shifted down.[4] The average is $(P_1 * Q_1 + P_2 * Q_2)/2$. With a buffer stock stabilization scheme, the buffer stock sells $Q_2 - Q_0$ units when the demand curve shifts down in order to keep the price at P_0. Whether the demand curve is shifted up or down, producers receive $P_0 * Q_0$ when the buffer stock operates, so this also is the value of their average revenues. Therefore price stabilization clearly implies producers' revenue stabilization in this case. But it also causes a reduction in the average value of producers' revenues since $P_0 * Q_0$ is smaller than $(P_1 * Q_1 + P_2 * Q_2)/2$, as can be seen by comparing in Fig. 3.1a the size of two rectangles each of which is $P_0 * Q_0$ with the sum of the areas in the rectangles that are $P_1 * Q_1$ and $P_2 * Q_2$. In the case of instability due to demands shifts alone, therefore, price stabilization causes producers' revenue stabilization, but at the cost of a reduction in those revenues.

Consider next the case of instability due to supply shifts alone. Here we must distinguish between various subcases that differ depending upon the supply and demand responsiveness to price changes. To summarize this price responsiveness it is useful to define the concept of elasticity. The price *elasticity of a curve* indicates by what percentage the quantity changes along a curve when the price changes by 1 percent. If the quantity changes by a

---

4 Here and below the standard notation of an "*" to mean multiplication is used. $P_1 * Q_1$, for example, should be read as P_1 multiplied by Q_1.

larger percentage than does the price, the absolute value[5] of the price elasticity for that curve is greater than one and the curve is price elastic for that range of price changes (for example, the demand curve and the supply curve in Fig. 3.1b). If the quantity changes by a smaller percentage than does the price, the absolute value of the price elasticity for that curve is less than one and the curve is price inelastic for that range of price changes (for example, the demand curve and the supply curve in Fig. 3.1c). If the quantity does not change at all when the price changes, the price elasticity is zero and the curve is completely price inelastic (for example, the supply curve in Fig. 3.1c).

Now let us consider the case of instability due to supply shifts alone. Johnson considers the most normal subcase to be one with price-elastic supply and demand curves (Fig. 3.1b). Following reasoning parallel to the case of demand shifts alone, we can find the average producers' revenues by considering what they are for both equally likely positions of the supply curve. Without price stabilization, producers' average revenues are $(P_2*Q_2 + P_3*Q_3)/2$. With stabilization they are $P_0*(Q_1 + Q_4)/2$. In this subcase price stabilization increases producers' revenues, as can be seen by comparing the sizes of the relevant rectangles once again.

What about the stability of revenues under price stabilization when supply curves alone shift? In the subcase of price-elastic supply and demand curves, price stabilization increases the instability of revenues.

Of course one also can consider mixed cases in which both demand and supply curves shift. The net result depends on the size of the two shifts and the size of the price elasticities. The tradeoff between level and instability of revenues nevertheless seems to persist in a number of theoretical cases.

Therefore Johnson concludes that price stabilization generally leads to a tradeoff between revenue stabilization and the level of revenues and that advocates of international commodity agreements lump together two different economic problems (instability of demand and instability of supply) that require quite different solutions. He is quite critical of the UNCTAD proposal and of the analysis underlying it.

Is Johnson right? This depends on exactly what are the objectives and what is the empirical reality regarding the relative importance of shifts in supply and demand and regarding the shapes of these curves. We can identify several subcases in which Johnson, not the advocates of international commodity agreements, apparently is wrong:

1. Suppose that, while the developing economies desire higher revenues, *ceteris paribus,*[6] they are *very* risk averse in wanting very much to avoid

---

5 We refer to the absolute value because normally along a demand curve the quantity changes in the opposite direction from the price, while along a supply curve both change in the same direction.

6 *Ceteris paribus* means "everything else being equal" or "everything else held constant."

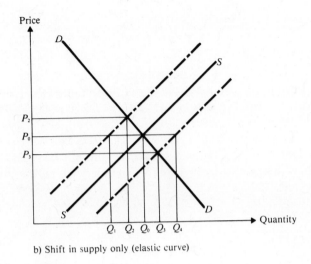

b) Shift in supply only (elastic curve)

Figure 3.1 [continued].

fluctuations in producers' revenues because of the perceived great disruptive effects of such fluctuations on their own economies. Then the proposal makes sense if either demand shifts dominate (Fig. 3.1a) or the curves are sufficiently inelastic (Fig. 3.1c).

2. Suppose that the objectives are weighted in the reverse order: While the developing countries would like revenue stabilization, they really care *much* more about increasing revenues. Then the proposal makes sense if shifts in supply curves are dominant (Figs. 3.1b-c). If the underlying curves are sufficiently price inelastic (Fig. 3.1c), moreover, producers' revenues may be increased at the same time fluctuations in those revenues are reduced.

3. Suppose that the assumptions of linear curves and/or parallel shifts are not valid. Then some of the conclusions of Johnson's "elementary economic analysis" may be changed. For example, consider the case in which the demand curve is very price inelastic above P_0 but very price elastic below this price and the completely price inelastic supply curve shifts (Fig. 3.2). Price stabilization may reduce revenues but increase their stability. This is the opposite outcome from what Johnson considers to be the normal result based on a shift in the supply curve with linear and price elastic curves (Fig. 3.1b).

4. Yet another possibility is that destabilizing speculation causes large price fluctuations that lower the long-run demand curve by inducing substitution of synthetics and other goods for the commodities of concern by risk-

---

7 Note that in the subcase of a supply shift and sufficiently price-inelastic curves, price stabilization leads to revenue stabilization and increased revenues (Fig. 3.1c).

averse manufacturers. Commodity producers, therefore, might rationally prefer price stabilization in order to limit the downward long-run shift in the market demand curve even if the short-term result may be lower immediate revenues or greater instability in revenues.

These possibilities all emphasize that in important respects the manner is an empirical question. Johnson's "elementary economic analysis" is not enough. Without empirical knowledge concerning preferences, long-run movements, the shapes of the curves, risk aversion, the elasticities, and the causes of shifts, whether they are additive or multiplicative, and so on, we cannot state with assurance what is the impact of price stabilization on producers' revenues.

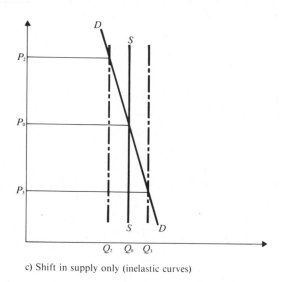

c) Shift in supply only (inelastic curves)

Figure 3.1 [continued].

At this point, it is useful to refer to some available empirical evidence: (1) For many of the relevant commodities, existing estimates indicate that short-run nonprice shifts in the supply curves tend to be larger than those in the demand curves, suggesting that Figs. 3.1b-c generally are more relevant than is Fig. 3.1a. (2) The estimated supply and demand price elasticities indicate for most of the relevant commodities quite low short-run price responsiveness. Therefore, the subcase of low price elasticities with price stabilization leading to larger revenues and less fluctuations in them (Fig. 3.1c) may be "normal," rather than the high price elasticities subcase with a tradeoff between the levels and instability of revenue (Fig. 3.1b) that Johnson emphasizes. (3) For foodgrains, Sarris, Abbott, and Taylor [2]

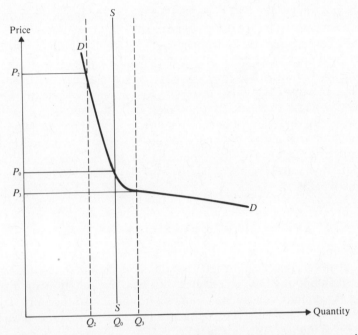

Fig. 3.2 Impact on producers' revenues of shift in inelastic supply curve with non-linear demand curve, with and without price stabilization at P_0 by a buffer stock

maintain that the nonlinear demand curve in Fig. 3.2 better represents reality than does the linear case.

And where does this empirical evidence lead us? For many of the UNCTAD core commodities it suggests that price stabilization may lead to revenue increases *and* greater revenue stability because of the dominance of supply shifts and low price elasticities. This may result in substantial benefits to the developing countries that, as a group, are net exporters of these commodities, independently of whether higher revenues or lower fluctuations in revenues are valued more highly. The possibility of forestalling long-run substitution for their exports by risk-averse users, also mentioned above, may increase the benefits of price stabilization to the developing countries.

For foodgrains, producers' revenues may be lowered, together with fluctuations therein, by price stabilization programs if Sarris, Abbott, and Taylor are right about the shape of the demand curve. However, Third World countries taken as a whole[8] still might benefit because they are net

---

8 A few developing countries (eg. Thailand, Burma, Argentina) are net exporters of foodgrains and thus, would not benefit under these assumptions.

importers of foodgrains. The lower level of producers' revenues in this case means lower consumer expenditures and import bills for them.

Thus, contrary to the assertions made by Johnson, simple economic theory in conjunction with this empirical evidence suggests that the developing countries as a whole well might benefit from effective price stabilization programs for many of the UNCTAD core commodities and for foodgrains. This is but a tentative conclusion, however, because we have not yet incorporated the dynamic adjustments of the interaction between supply and demand into our analysis. We return to such questions in Chapter 5, where we simulate the impact of price stabilization programs with models that incorporate empirical estimates of the relevant elasticities and of the dynamic adjustment paths.

3.2 WHO GAINS FROM PRICE STABILIZATION?

This question is related to the subject of the previous section, but the impact on consumers also needs to be incorporated. We explore it here under simplifying assumptions that ignore risk aversion, the question of distributional effects among consumers or among producers, storage and transaction costs for the buffer stock, and general-equilibrium aspects outside of the market of interest. We measure the benefits (losses) to producers by the additional (lessened) revenues they receive. We measure the benefits (losses) to consumers by the additional (lessened) consumer surplus they receive.

Consumer surplus is measured by the sum, for all units of a commodity, of the difference between what consumers would be willing to pay for each unit and what they have to pay. To illustrate, consider the downward sloping demand curve in Fig. 3.3. To purchase the first unit consumers are willing to pay a price P_3. To purchase the next unit they are willing to pay a price slightly less than P_3. To purchase the Q_2th unit they are willing to pay P_2. If the market price is P_2, then P_2 must be paid for each of the Q_2 units demanded. To measure the consumer surplus given a market price of P_2, we subtract P_2 from what consumers would be willing to pay for each of the Q_2 units actually purchased. But that is just the difference between the demand curve and the horizontal price line at P_2, or the area indicated by the triangle labeled J in Fig. 3.3. Likewise, with a market price of P_0, the consumer surplus would be $J + F + G$.

Now let us return to the question of who gains and who loses from price stabilization. Let us consider the case in Fig. 3.3 in which the completely price inelastic supply curve is equally likely to be at Q_1 or Q_2, so on average it is at Q_0. Assume that the demand curve is fixed, so the only source of instability is the shifting supply curve. P_0 is the average price and the one at which the buffer stock stabilizes the price when it is in operation.

When the supply curve shifts out to Q_1, the buffer stock purchases $Q_1 - Q_0$ units. The change in consumer surplus due to paying P_0 instead of

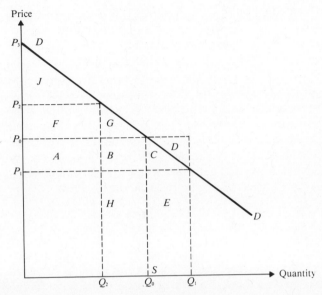

Fig. 3.3 Gains and losses from price stabilization (shifts in inelastic supply curve only)

the price P_1 that would have prevailed without a buffer stock is negative, $- A - B - C$. The producers' revenue gain due to the higher prices is positive, $A + B + C + D$. The cost to the buffer stock of purchasing $Q_1 - Q_0$ units is $- C - D - E$. The total benefit (summing these three components) is $- C - E$.

When the supply curve shifts to Q_2, $Q_0 - Q_2$ units are sold by the buffer stock at price P_0. This precludes the price from rising to P_2, as it otherwise would. The benefit to the consumers is $F + G$ due to the lower price and the larger quantity. The benefit to the producers is $- F$ since they receive a lower price for their Q_2 units than they would without the buffer stock. The financial inflow to the buffer stock is $B + H$. The total benefit is the sum of these three components, $B + G + H$.

If the sequencing over time of the supply shifts is ignored,[9] the total benefits to each of the three groups is the sum of those obtained from buffer stock operation with supply at Q_1 and at Q_2. For consumers the sum is $F + G - A - B - C$. For producers the sum is $A + B + C + D - F$. For the buffer stock the sum is $B + H - C - D - E$. For the total benefit the sum is $B + G + H - C - E$. Under these assumptions the sum for the buffer

---

9 In Section 5.1 we discuss how events in the distant future might be discounted to make them comparable to current events. In the terminology of that discussion, we here are assuming a zero discount rate.

stock is zero and the overall sum is positive.[10] However, whether or not consumers or producers, respectively, benefit depends on the exact shape of the curves. The issue basically is an empirical one.

The thoughtful reader will realize that Fig. 3.3 represents only one of the alternative cases and subcases considered in the previous section. We could examine each of these and others in which the curves are not linear or the shifts are not parallel. To do so would only reinforce the conclusion that either the producers or the consumers might gain, but the issue is basically empirical. Instead of examining each theoretical possibility, therefore, in Chapters 5 and 6 we focus on the gains that are implied by the empirical estimates of actual supply and demand curves for the commodities of interest.

3.3 NORMATIVE IMPLICATIONS OF MARKET SOLUTIONS[11]

Pure competition is defined to be the situation in which no single participant has the capacity to affect market prices more than infinitesimaly (in other words, no single participant has market power). From the point of view of individual entities in the market place, prices seem to be given (not necessarily fixed over time) parameters independent of their own behavior. Pure competition generally is considered an interesting paradigm for reasons summarized below, but not of very general applicability in the real world. However, most of the initial producers of agricultural commodities that enter into international commodity markets (and agricultural products account for about 85 percent of total nonpetroleum commodity exports from developing countries) and most of the ultimate consumers (generally in processed form of both the agricultural and nonagricultural internationally traded commodities sell and purchase these goods, respectively, under conditions approximating pure competition. At both ends of the marketchain for the relevant international commodities (but not in the middle, where marketing boards, other government agencies, and large companies dominate), therefore, the purely competitive model has substantial applicability.

What are the advantages of pure competition? Some answers are in the area of political economy and thus derivative of particular value systems. Under pure competition the basic economic problems (for example, what is produced, how is it produced, and for whom is it produced) are solved in an

---

10 To see this, note in Fig. 3.3 that $B + H = C + D + E$ (so the sum for the buffer stock is zero) and $B + G + H$ is greater than $C + E$ (so the total benefit is positive).

11 The distinction often is made between positive and normative economics. Positive economic analysis reveals what happens under certain conditions (for example, if the demand curve is downward sloping, the quantity demanded declines as the price increases, everything else held constant). Normative economics pertains to what should occur, and, therefore, incorporates value judgments. Appendix A provides a more detailed analysis of the issues in this section for the interested reader.

impersonal manner, independently of personal ties or characteristics such as race or national origin.[12] The atomistic structure of buyers and sellers required for competition also decentralizes and disperses power. Moreover, if the conditions necessary for pure competition to exist do in fact prevail, freedom of entry into various industries and individual mobility will both be high.

In response to the question about the advantages of pure competition, most economists focus on answers related to economic efficiency. In a world with the correct initial distribution of input ownership for a given social welfare function, with easy entry (for instance, due to a lack of legal restrictions and limited increasing returns to scale relative to the size of industries), with no externalities, with no uncertainty, and with pure competition everywhere else, pure competition in international commodity markets results in maximization of the social welfare function.[13]

This is a strong result. But what does it really mean? Appendix A explores this questions in some depth, and interested readers are encouraged to study it for more details. Here it suffices to expand on the notion of efficiency by distinguishing among efficiency in production, efficiency in exchange, and overall efficiency. Under the assumptions of the previous paragraph, pure competition leads to all three kinds of efficiency, as well as to maximization of social welfare.

Efficiency in production occurs if production of one good cannot be increased without lessening the production of some other good. That is, the economy is on the production frontier of Fig. 1.1 so that no more manufactured products can be made without reducing the output of agricultural products (or vice versa). Under pure competition each firm chooses to sell the number of units of product at which its marginal cost (the cost of producing the last unit) just equals the market price of the product in order to maximize its profits. Also, each firm selects its inputs so that the marginal products (i.e. the additional products obtained from using the last units of inputs) for the last dollars spent on all inputs are identical in order to minimize the costs of producing the profit-maximizing level of output. This means that an individual firm satisfying this condition could not gain by substituting one input for another. It also means that society as a whole could not increase the output of one good without reducing the output of some other good since every firm minimizes its cost by equalizing across inputs the marginal product for the last dollar spent on each input and every firm faces the same input prices. The last unit of each input is everywhere valued the same, so no overall output increase can result from merely shifting inputs around. Such behavior assures efficiency in production.

---

12 Given certain sets of values, this impersonality is a negative dehumanizing feature.

13 The assumptions made here are defined and discussed below.

Efficiency in exchange means that for a given level of production of all goods, no one individual can be made better off merely by exchanging goods with someone else without making at least one other person worse off. Under pure competition all individuals maximize their satisfactions (or utilities) by choosing a combination of goods so that the last bit of satisfaction (that is, marginal utility) obtained from the last dollar spent on the good is the same for all goods. Since every person faces the same product prices, every person values the last unit of one good that they purchase relative to the last unit of another in the same relative way. Therefore everyone could not be made better off merely by switching given levels of goods among individuals. Such behavior assures efficiency in exchange.

Overall efficiency exists when the rate at which the last unit of product of one good can be transformed into another by moving along the production possibility frontier is the same as the rate of which individuals substitute the last unit of one good for the other. The rate at which the last unit of one commodity can be transformed into the other is given by the ratio of the marginal costs of the two commodities, or the slope of the production possibility frontier. Given that purely competitive firms choose an output at which the marginal cost is equal to the product price, this rate of transformation between two goods is equal to the ratio of the product prices. But satisfaction-maximizing consumers also choose combinations of goods so that their ratios of marginal satisfactions (or marginal utilities) are equal to these same ratios of product prices. Marginal consumption decisions among goods are made on the basis of true relative marginal costs of production for society. Therefore, pure competition assures overall efficiency. In such a situation no one can be made better off—by changing inputs among firms, by changing the composition of output among commodities, or by changing the distribution of output among consumers—without making someone else worse off.

Social welfare maximization occurs if there is a social welfare function that depends on the levels of satisfactions of all individuals and if the maximum value of this function is obtained for a given supply of inputs, technology, and preferences of individuals. Given any particular social welfare function, pure competition leads to its maximization if there is overall efficiency *and* if the initial ownership of inputs is exactly right so that the market solutions lead to just the right incomes for that particular social welfare function.[14]

---

14 For example, if the social welfare function weighted everyone's preferences equally, a very unequal distribution of ownership of inputs probably would not lead to maximization of the function. On the other hand, if the socal welfare function put very high weight on the satisfaction of one individual, it probably would not be maximized by an equal distribution of ownership of inputs.

Reservations

The result that pure competition leads to social welfare maximization is a strong result. But the necessary conditions are very strong too, and obviously not even approximately satisfied in the real world. Let us consider them one by one.

First, maximization of a social welfare function depends upon having exactly the right distribution of income and therefore of ownership of inputs. Within a static framework, much of the conflict between the developing and developed nations may arise at this point. Even if all the other conditions given above are satisfied so that economic efficiency is attained, the initial distribution of assets is seen by many to be so inequitable that the world is far away from a welfare maximization. Efficiency concerns may be unimportant in light of this maldistribution.

Second, leaving aside the question of welfare maximization, pure competition leads to overall efficiency if all of the other conditions are satisfied. No shift in resources and so on exists that would improve the welfare of any one individual without reducing the welfare of at least one other individual. Attainment of this state seems desirable, everything else being equal, and its virtues are emphasized (perhaps overemphasized) by many economists. But the existence of pure competition alone is not enough to guarantee even efficiency. To obtain efficiency in the above discussion we had to assume that there are no externalities. That is, we had to assume that the production of one product depends only on the market inputs used directly in the production process for it and that the utility of an individual depends only on the market goods he or she consumes. In the real world, however, externalities abound. Individuals' satisfactions depend not only on their consumption of purchased items, but also on such factors as the consumption of others (for example, "keeping up with the Jones") or non-market products like pollution. Likewise, production of one good may depend not only on the inputs purchased for use in its production process, but also on other nonmarket factors such as pollution. The existence of these nonmarket interdependencies or externalities precludes overall efficiency even if the conditions exist to permit pure competition.

Third, even if all of the conditions for the existence of pure competition are satisfied and there are no externalities, the behavioral assumptions assumed above may not be satisfied. For example, it is assumed that firms maximize profits. But firms may have other objectives or considerations in mind. Possibilities include avoiding risk in an uncertain world or providing perquisites (such as nice offices and company cars) for the managers. If such other considerations are important, behavior of these firms may not be approximated well by profit maximization—and efficient outcomes do not result.

Fourth, the conditions for pure competition to exist often are not satisfied even if profit maximization and the lack of externalities are both assumed. Entry into an industry is not easy in many cases due to legal, natural, and technological monopolies or due to increasing returns to scale that are large relative to the industry. If there are relatively few firms in an industry, they perceive correctly that they have market power in that they can affect their product price by changing their output. Fig. 3.4 illustrates the profit-maximizing behavior of a monopolist in the M industry. Since the demand curve is sloping downward, to sell more the monopolist must lower the price. As a result, the marginal revenue (or additional revenue generated from selling one more unit) is below the demand curve since the price must be lowered on all previous units to sell one more unit. The profit-maximizing level of output is M_1, at which level the marginal revenue equals the marginal cost.[15] At lower outputs the marginal revenue exceeds the marginal cost, so profits can be increased by expanding output and sales (and vice versa at higher levels of output). To sell M_1 units of output, the monopolist must charge the price PM_1, as is indicated by the demand curve. But this profit-maximizing condition for the monopolist implies a price greater than marginal cost. Therefore, if industry A is purely competitive and industry M is a monopoly, the economy no longer satisfies the overall efficiency condition. Instead, people are substituting between A and M at the margin at a different rate than the relative marginal cost of A to M.

Let us pursue one implication of this example further. Ignore the possibilities of externalities for the moment and presume that the only nonpure competition in the system is the existence of monopoly in the production and sale of M. To obtain overall efficiency, the "first best" solution would be to make M act as a pure competitor, perhaps by breaking it up into enough small units so that none has perceptible influence on the market price. But suppose that such an option is not available? What is best to do? Under the assumptions we have made, the "second-best" solution is for A to charge the same ratio of price to marginal cost as does M. Then the overall efficiency condition is satisfied.

This is an illustration of the "theory of second best": If all of the conditions for an optimum cannot be satisfied, efficient outcomes can be ensured by introducing particular new distortions. The problem is that the desirable new distortions depend on the exact nature of the particular situation. The second-best solution indicated in the previous paragraph, for example, works under the particular assumptions indicated, but would not be efficient if one or both industries produced inputs for the other or if total vari-

---

15 The next section discusses the case of limit pricing to preclude entry by firms with market power, in which case the optimal strategy may not be to maximize short-run profits.

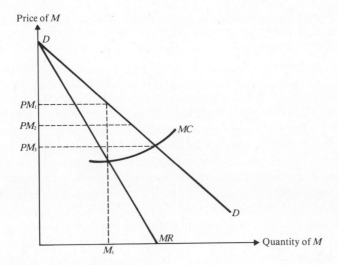

Fig. 3.4 Market behavior of a monopoly

able input supplies were not fixed. Thus, to devise second-best solutions in the real world requires much more knowledge than policy-makers normally have.

What does this discussion of the possibility of nonpurely competitive markets mean in the consideration of international commodity markets? Clearly, substantial market power exists in markets other than the commodity markets in the real world. In principle, if such market power in the rest of the world cannot be eliminated, in the interests of efficiency the theory of the second-best suggests that it *might* be desirable to introduce it into international markets (if it does not already exist), not resist interfering in these markets because of supposed advantages of pure competition!

Realistically, substantial market power already exists in most international commodity markets. In the majority of cases, a relatively few buyers (governments or large firms) account for most of the purchases. In many cases sales are also quite concentrated. If there is no new attempt to regulate these markets, therefore, the alternatives are not an efficient, purely competitive system as many of the critics of the international commodity agreements seem to assume, but systems with considerable existing market imperfections.

Fifth, the whole analysis above is at a point of time without uncertainty. Incorporation of risk aversion and dynamic considerations well might vitiate the claim that pure competition leads to efficient outcomes over time. Schumpeter, for example, placed great emphasis on the importance of market power to lead to new technological developments that are much more important in a dynamic context than is static efficiency (see Behrman [3]). Although such claims are not uncontested, the possibility that they are right raises further doubts about advocating unregulated markets on short-run efficiency grounds above.

Conclusion

Where does this discussion leave us? Unhindered markets may be relatively efficient devices for processing a great deal of information to signal shortages or surpluses through price or inventory changes. However, one has to be quite careful in regard to their normative implications. They lead to maximization of a given social welfare function only with the correct distribution of assets and the satisfaction of all of the other conditions discussed above. They lead to economic efficiency only under strong and unrealistic assumptions. The "theory of second best" at worst implies that, in the real world, policies directed at economic efficiency should be abandoned. At best it suggests the advocation of "third-best," very general, policies that have a reasonable probability of leading to greater economic efficiency but that do not guarantee a step in that direction when applied in a specific case. Dynamic considerations may weaken further the argument for unhindered markets leading to overall efficiency.

Economic theory leads us to this highly qualified view of the normative properties of unhindered market solutions. It is a much weaker view than that of many who oppose international commodity agreements on the basis that they would lessen the gains from free market operations. One can understand why economists from developing countries might wonder if the position of the strongest advocates of unhindered free market operations is based on a lack of understanding of underlying economic theory, or a disguised defense of vested interests in the status quo.

3.4 CONDITIONS UNDER WHICH COLLUSIVE ACTION BY PRODUCERS ALONE CAN RAISE MARKET PRICES

The basic motivation behind the advocacy of international commodity agreements may have little to do with stabilization per se. Instead, the major concern may be to raise the real resources of the developing countries who export the affected commodities. Under certain conditions discussed in Section 3.1 above (for example, dominant supply shifts), stabilization itself may lead to increased revenues for the exporters. The content of the UNCTAD documents, however, suggests that the concern goes further than this to a desire to raise market prices (or prevent real market prices from falling) to levels above that which otherwise would prevail. If market demand curves are price inelastic, successful price raising is rewarded by greater revenues since the quantities demanded do not decline by as large a percentage as prices rise.

This leads us into a much less rigorous area of economic theory: oligopoly formation and behavior. An oligopoly is an industry than has a small number of producers. Each member of an oligopoly can perceive that not only does its own output decision affect the market price, but also the output decisions of all its fellow oligopolists affect the market price. This interdependency creates a rivalry (although not necessarily price competition) among the oligopolists in regard to the division of the existing market. If the oligopolists are able to agree how to divide the market shares, they can maximize their joint profits by acting as a monopolist and selecting that output for which industry marginal cost is equal to marginal revenue (M_1 in Fig. 3.4).

However, this is a very static view. If the oligopolists collude to raise prices, new firms may be induced to enter into the industry or new substitutes may be developed to compete with the product of the industry. This brings us to the possibility of limit pricing to discourage entry. In Fig. 3.4 the collusive short-run static profit-maximizing price is PM_1. Suppose, however, that at any price above PM_2, new entrants are induced. To maximize long-run profits it may be desirable from the point of view of the colluding oligopolists to set the price below the short-run profit maximizing level in order to limit the inducement for new firms to enter. The effective long-run demand curve for the current colluding oligopolists has a horizontal segment at PM_2 until it hits the downward-sloping demand curve DD. The colluders have to decide how to balance off higher short-run and long-run prices and profits. The easier is entry or the possibility of others substituting for the product, the less are the colluding oligopolists able both to gain large current profits and to maintain longer-run market power.

The theory of limit pricing and a number of theories[16] of how oligopolists divide a given market share lead to a checklist of conditions that seem to facilitate oligopolistic coordination of pricing and output decisions: (1) the perception that joint action will lead to greater returns for producers, (2) common output preferences due to similar cost structures and market shares, (3) cheap and rapid communication, (4) high concentration of production in relatively few firms, (5) a small (or no) competitive fringe, (6) repetitive small transactions, (7) homogeneity and simplicity of products, (8) the willingness to utilize inventory and order backlogs as buffers instead of making overly sensitive price adjustments, (9) limited or no substitution for the product, and (10) high barriers to entry (for example, restricted technological knowledge, restricted control over exhaustible resources, legal re-

---

16 See any standard intermediate economic theory or industrial organization textbook. None of these theories is completely persuasive.

strictions on new firms, returns to scale at a high level of production relative to market size).

How do the UNCTAD core commodities stack up against such a checklist? In some respects they do rather well: product homogeneity, frequent transactions, and a common perceived interest—at least currently among the developing country producers. But in other respects they generally fare poorly: low barriers to entry, limited returns to scale, an active competitive fringe, substantial current and potential substitution for the products. And for the commodity that probably is most promising by these criteria—copper—the developing countries account for about only 40 percent of world production. Thus the developing countries indeed may be advocating international commodity agreements that include both producers and consumers because they perceive little likelihood of developing successful producer cartels for the ten core commodities on their own. In an important sense, therefore, the oil cartel of OPEC may seem *not* to be a model that can be imitated by producers of the UNCTAD core commodities.

3.5 CONCLUSIONS

The theoretical considerations of this chapter give important insights into the arguments for and against international commodity agreements. They suggest that the developing-country producers of the ten UNCTAD core commodities may be advocating such agreements because the chances of success of producers' cartels for these commodities are not high. They also indicate that normative arguments against international commodity agreements on the grounds of efficiency or social welfare maximization are *not* well based. Finally, they imply that whether producers or consumers gain from international commodity agreements and whether or not there is a tradeoff between the level and instability of producers' revenues cannot be established on the basis of economic theory. Instead, empirical analysis is required. The rest of this book attempts to provide such analysis.

REFERENCES

1. H. G. Johnson. "Commodities: Less Developed Countries' Demands and Developed Countries Response." Paper presented at MIT Workshop on Specific Proposals and Desirable DC Response to LDC Demands Regarding the New International Economic Order, 17-20 May 1976.

2. A. H. Sarris, P. Abbott, and L. Taylor. *World Grain Reserves*. Washington, D. C.: Overseas Development Council, 1977.

3. J. R. Behrman. "Development Economics." *Modern Economic Thought*. Ed. by S. Weintraub. Philadelphia: University of Pennsylvania Press, 1977.

Historical Experience in   *4*
International Commodity Markets: Price Fluctuations, Price Trends, and Previous Commodity Agreements

The previous chapter presented theoretical analysis of various aspects of international commodity agreements, such as proposed by UNCTAD. We now turn to the historical experience in international commodity markets to give us further insight about such agreements. Section 4.1 examines the degrees of fluctuations in these markets in the past quarter century. Section 4.2 investigates the secular trends in commodity prices over the same time period. Section 4.3 considers the experience with previous international commodity agreements and producer cartels. Section 4.4 gives conclusions.

4.1 FLUCTUATIONS IN INTERNATIONAL COMMODITY MARKETS

Price movements in any historical period may be decomposed into two components: the secular or long-run trend and variations from the secular trend. Fig. 4.1 provides an illustration using the World Bank index of terms of trade for nonpetroleum primary commodities in the 1954-1975 period. The dashed line is the secular tendency in this index. The solid line gives actual movements in the index. The variations of the actual prices (solid line) around the secular trend (dashed line) reflect short-run fluctuations in the index.

One major objective of most international commodity agreements, and of the UNCTAD IV resolution in particular, is price stabilization. Possible motives for having price stabilization as a major goal include: (1) limiting the inducements for substituting synthetics for natural products due to risk aversion on the part of users in developed economies, especially in the cases of jute, sisal, rubber, and cotton; (2) lessening the negative effects of revenue fluctuations on the developing economies due to risk aversion and costs that originate in uncertainty (but Section 3.1 points out that price stabiliza-

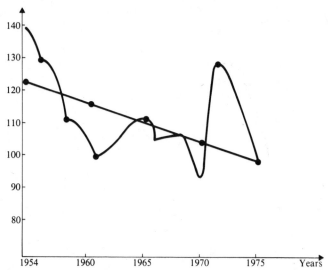

Fig. 4.1 The World Bank index of the terms of trade of primary commodities, 1954-1975*

tion may not imply revenue stabilization if supply fluctuations are dominant); (3) increasing the probability of the cooperation of consuming nations, who historically have focused much more on the question of stability (Section 4.3), in schemes the primary purpose of which is to increase export revenues of the developing countries either by price stabilization when fluctuations originate primarily on the supply side (Section 3.1) or by increasing the price with a price-inelastic demand curve.

This section considers empirical evidence related to historical fluctuations in prices and revenues. The next section explores the historical price trends.

Fig. 4.1 gives some idea of the deviations from the secular trend for a weighted average of the terms of trade of thirty-four important nonpetroleum primary commodity exports from the developing countries. The fluctuations seem to be fairly large. Consider, for example, the movement from the trough in 1972 to the peak in 1974.

But there are even larger fluctuations for individual commodity prices, which partially cancel out in the construction of the aggregate index. And most developing economies specialize in a few, or even just one, of these primary commodities. Therefore, it is instructive to consider the fluctuations for the individual commodities.

* The World Bank index of primary commodity terms of trade is based on unit values of developing countries' exports of thirty-four nonpetroleum primary commodities. The index is weighted by 1967-1969 values of these exports and is deflated by the World Bank's index of prices of manufactured goods in world trade. *Source:* Hansen, et. al. [1]. The secular tendency is estimated as is discussed in Appendix B.

Columns 4-6 of Table 4.1 present indices of fluctuations (the mean absolute percentage deviation from the time trends) for market prices, value, and deflated value over the 1953-1972 period for the seventeen commodities included in the UNCTAD [2] proposal. For some of these commodities, international agreements were in effect for part of this period. The evidence reviewed in Section 4.3, however, suggests that such agreements did not generally reduce price instability.

Table 4.1 Rates of growth and fluctuations in prices and values of UNCTAD core and other commodities

	Rates of growth 1953-1972			Indices of fluctuations 1953-1972*		
	Market prices	Value	Deflated value†	Market prices	Value	Deflated value†
	(Percent per annum)			(Percent)		
1.Core commodities	(1)	(2)	(3)	(4)	(5)	(6)
Coffee	−1.6	1.0	−0.4	17.0	11.1	9.2
Cocoa	−1.3	1.7	0.2	23.0	13.4	12.6
Tea	−1.9	0.0	−1.5	6.2	5.5	6.0
Sugar	0.2	3.8	2.2	33.4	9.2	7.5
Cotton	−0.7	1.1	−0.4	8.2	9.1	7.9
Rubber	−3.2	−1.7	−3.1	13.2	14.7	14.4
Jute‡‡	1.9	0.7	−0.8	11.9	12.2	14.1
Sisal	−1.2	−0.3	−1.8	18.0	26.3	28.6
Copper	4.0	7.8	6.2	21.5	17.1	17.5
Tin	4.0	5.2	3.6	7.9	18.8	18.4
2.Other commodities						
Wheat	–	−2.8	−4.2	4.7	28.6	31.1
Rice	0.5	0.3	−1.2	11.3	12.9	14.8
Bananas	−0.9	3.9	2.4	4.3	7.7	7.2
Beef and veal§	6.9	12.0	10.3	20.8	15.4	15.1
Wool	−2.2	−3.6	−5.0	11.4	10.2	12.5
Bauxite‖	2.6	8.1	6.5	4.7	8.8	10.8
Iron ore	−2.4	9.3	7.7	8.3	10.8	12.3
TOTAL	–	–	–	–	–	–

Source: UNCTAD [4]

*The fluctuation index is the average over the period of differences between annual observations and calculated trend values (irrespective of sign) expressed as percentages of the trend value.
†Export value deflated by UN unit value index for world exports of manufactured goods.
‡Including jute manufactures.
§Including cattle.
‖"Prices" are export unit values; value in 1972 includes alumina.

In regard to price fluctuations, the statistics in this table suggest a variety of experiences for different commodities. The ten core commodities divide into three groups: high price instability (sugar, cocoa, and copper); moderate price instability (sisal, coffee, rubber, and jute); and low price instability (cotton, tin, and tea). The other seven commodities included in the UNCTAD proposal fall into the moderate (wool, rice, and possibly beef and veal) or low (iron ore, wheat, bauxite, and bananas) price instability categories. Related indices presented in Behrman [3] for fifteen other important primary commodity exports from the developing countries include two (i.e. linseed oil and zinc) in the high category and the rest in the middle or low categories. Thus the UNCTAD "core" commodities do include a fairly large representation of ones that have experienced relatively high price instability in the past quarter century.[1] And average annual fluctuations of 10, 20 or 30 percent indeed would seem to make planning difficult for individual producers and users and for governments.

Three questions about this historical experience naturally arise: (1) Why have some commodities experienced relatively high price instability? (2) What has price instability implied for revenue instability? (3) Has instability been concentrated more among developing than developed countries? Each of these questions are now considered in turn.

Causes of Differential Price Instability

Within the simple supply-demand market model discussed in Section 3.1 and presented in Fig. 3.1, instability is greater the less are the price elasticities[2] of supply and of demand, the more the supply and demand schedules shift in the price-quantity plane, and the less those shifts are positively correlated.[3]

On the bases of the average of the absolute short-run supply and demand price elasticities in columns 1 and 3 of Table 5.1, the seven commodities in the low price instability group (tin, bauxite, wheat, iron ore, cotton, bananas, and tea) rank 1, 2, 3, 4-5, 4-5, 7-9, and 13-16. The three commodities in the high price instability group (copper, cocoa, and sugar) rank 10, 11-12, and 13-16. Therefore, although there are exceptions such as tea, the

---

1 Recently some of the price fluctuations have been quite considerable. UNCTAD [5] gives examples of the peak 1974 monthly price exceeding the 1973 average price by 70 percent for copper, 58 percent for rubber, and 53 percent for cotton. By April 1975, moreover, the prices had fallen to 44, 50, and 55 percent, respectively, of the 1974 peaks.

2 Price elasticities are defined in Section 3.1.

3 That is, the less the curves shift together. If both curves shift to the right by the same distance, no matter how big the shift, the equilibrium price is not affected. If one shifts to the right and the other to the left, however, even small shifts may cause large changes in the equilibrium price.

association between price inelasticity and price instability seems quite strong. The role of price inelasticities in creating relatively great price instability for the group as a whole also is apparent in that for only two of the seventeen commodities (tin and bauxite) does the sum of the absolute values of the short-run supply and demand price elasticities exceed one.

It is more difficult to find systematic information about the relative extent and coordination of supply and demand shifts across the seventeen commodities. The income elasticities of demand in column 4 of Table 5.1 provide a measure of the extent of sensitivity across commodities to one possible source of instability in the price quantity plane, fluctuations in income in the consuming countries. Analogous to the definition of price elasticity in Section 3.1, the income elasticity of demand is defined as the percentage change in quantity demanded for a given percentage change in income with all other relevant variables, including price, held constant. High income elasticities imply that the demand curve shifts relatively a lot in the price-quantity plane, everything else being equal, and vice versa. Four of the low price instability groups do have low income elasticities, which would seem to contribute to price stability. However, the others have high income elasticities, and the high price instability groups are not concentrated in any part of the ranking by income elasticities. Thus the association between income elasticities and price instabilities is much less definite than the association discussed in the previous paragraph between price inelasticities and price instabilities.

Unfortunately there is no easy way to explore the sensitivity across these commodities to other variables that might shift the supply and/or demand curves, such as weather conditions, labor market disruptions, and political events.

As is emphasized in Chapter 3, the simple analysis of supply and demand curves cannot tell the whole story about international commodity markets. During the past quarter century there have been a number of nonpurely competitive activities in international commodity markets that may have affected price stability.

One group of such activities is the operation of international commodity agreements. Such agreements were in effect for substantial parts of the period for tin, wheat, and sugar, and less so for coffee. The first two of these commodities are in the low instability group, sugar is in the high instability group, and coffee is in between. As is discussed in Section 4.3, it is inappropriate to conclude that the degree of price stability reflected primarily operations of the international agreements. Far more important for tin and wheat were another set of nonpurely competitive activities: United States (and Canadian for wheat) stockpiling and sales outside of the agreements. For sugar, the Cuban-United States-Union of Soviet Socialist Republic conflict exacerbated instability in a case where the international free market is very narrow due to many government regulations and trade arrangements that fragment the total world market.

Another nonpurely competitive factor that may have been relevant for some of these commodities is the operation of highly vertically integrated oligopolistic firms.[4] Such firms may have increased price stability for two reasons: (1) because of the willingness of oligopolistic producers to make quantity adjustments instead of price adjustments in order to maintain industry price discipline, and (2) because such prices may have been used primarily for internal bookkeeping purposes or to avoid taxes in a particular country,[5] rather than for resource allocation. The commodities most characterized by a high degree of vertical integration among oligopolistic firms for most of the past quarter century are bananas, bauxite, and, somewhat less so, iron ore and copper. The first three of these in fact are in the low price instability group. Copper is not, but probably did experience relatively little price instability before the mid-1960s. Subsequently the vertical integration in copper was effectively broken down, first by new pricing policies encouraged by the international copper-producing countries' organization and then by nationalizations of copper production in developing countries.

Revenue Stability

As is discussed in Section 3.1, commodity agreements focus on price stabilization, which may or may not lead to the revenue stabilization of more interest. Column 5 in Table 4.1 presents indices of fluctuations in revenue over the 1953-1972 period. Comparison of column 5 with the indices of price fluctuations in column 4 reveals that for five of the ten core commodities (coffee, cocoa, tea, sugar, and copper) and two of the other seven commodities (beef and veal, and wool), movements in quantities were partially compensating. Therefore, mean percentage absolute fluctuations from the trends in revenues were less in magnitude than mean percentage absolute fluctuations from the trends in prices. For the other five core commodities and the remaining five other commodities, prices and quantities tended to

---

4 Section 3.4 considers some important aspects of oligopolistic behavior.

5 Suppose that a vertically integrated firm mines or grows a primary commodity in one country and processes it and sells it in another. By increasing the price it charges itself for the unprocessed product in the first country, it can lower its recorded net revenues and income tax obligation in the second country and increase both in the first (or vice versa). If the tax rates are higher in the second country, it may choose to record higher prices for the raw material in order to lower its overall tax obligation (or vice versa). If such a motivation explains the level of the recorded price for the transfer internal to the firm, it is not liable to lead to frequent fluctuations in the recorded internal price of the raw material.

move together more so that the mean percentage absolute fluctuations in values exceed those in prices.

In the first group the differences between the price and value indices of fluctuation are particularly large for sugar, cocoa, and tea. In the second group the differences are particularly large for wheat, tin, and sisal. For these six commodities, apparently the quantity fluctuations were relatively large.

As a result of differential quantity adjustments, the ordering by revenue instability differs in some significant respects from that for price instability. Among the ten core commodities, revenue instability in real terms (column 6 in Table 4.1) is high for sisal; medium for tin, copper, rubber, jute, and cocoa; and low for coffee, cotton, sugar, and tea. Among the seven other commodities, it is high for wheat; medium for beef and veal, rice, wool, iron ore, and bauxite; and low for bananas. Of the three commodities in the high price instability category, none remains there for revenue instability. Cocoa and copper are in the middle group for revenue instability and sugar is in the low group. Of the seven commodities in the low price instability category, only tea, cotton, and bananas remain there for revenue instability. Tin, iron ore, and bauxite are in the middle category for revenue instability, and wheat is in the high category.

There is another aspect of the changes between price instability and revenue instability that merits mention. There seems to be some relation between the relative size of the price versus value instability indices and at least one form of nonpurely competitive market activity mentioned above. For each of the three cases of oligopolistic vertically integrated industries with low price instability noted above (bananas, bauxite, and iron ore), the index of fluctuations in value exceeds that of fluctuations in price. This is consistent with more reliance on quantity as opposed to price adjustments in response to changed market conditions, a type of behavior characteristic of colluding oligopolistic firms.

For another type of nonpurely competitive market organization mentioned above—the maintenance of international commodity agreements—no pattern is obvious. For wheat and tin, prices did not fluctuate much around the trend, but revenues were quite volatile. For sugar and coffee, the reverse held.

Finally, note that revenues have fluctuated substantially around the trend for many of these commodities. For twelve of the seventeen commodities, deviations from the trend of real revenues average over 10 percent per year. Such fluctuations may make planning difficult and have a high cost in terms of risk aversion for producers and users. That half of these twelve commodities are not in the core group, however, again suggests that stabilization is not the only objective of the UNCTAD commodity proposal.

Concentration of Instabilities among Exports of Developing Countries

It has been almost an article of faith among many policy-makers and econo-mists in the developing nations that the developing countries suffer particu-larly violent fluctuations in their export earnings due to their concentration on primary exports. Although developing countries account for only about one-third of world nonpetroleum commodity exports, such exports account for a substantial portion (about 55 percent) of the nonpetroleum exports from the developing countries. But that primary commodity exports are very important to developing nations and that revenues from individual commodity exports are quite volatile is not a sufficient basis on which to conclude that the export earnings of the developing countries are relatively volatile because of their concentration on primary commodities. Fluctua-tions may partially cancel out across the various commodities that deter-mine the export earnings of a particular country.

In the early 1960s, several cross-country studies questioned many of the assumptions underlying the traditional explanations for the causes of export earnings instability. The general conclusion of these studies is that export earnings instability is at most weakly associated with (1) the proportion of primary products in the export mix, (2) the degree of commodity concentra-tion, and (3) the geographic concentration of the export market. They also found that the developing countries do not experience a great deal more ex-port instability than do the developed countries.

Subsequent studies for more recent periods, however, report instabili-ties in export earnings for developing countries substantially larger than for developed economies. And even these more recent studies do not incorpor-ate the commodity price boom and bust of the 1970s, during which period the relative volatility in export earnings for developing nations probably in-creased. The later studies also tend to bring into question some of the con-clusions of the earlier work on the causes of export instability. Recent work, for example, reports a significant relation between export concentration and export instability. Still, the variables relating to the commodity compo-sition of exports appear to be proxies for country-specific characteristics of both the country of origin and the country of destination.

At this point in time, therefore, support seems fairly strong for the pro-position that developing countries recently have experienced greater insta-bility in their export earnings than have more developed countries. Consid-erable uncertainty remains about the role of dependence on primary com-modities in this instability.

4.2 SECULAR TRENDS IN INTERNATIONAL COMMODITY PRICES

The second major objective of many international commodity agreements, including the UNCTAD [6] proposal, is to improve the secular trend of commodity prices. By the secular trend, once again, we mean the long-run tendency, as is represented by the dashed line in Fig. 4.1. Indexation of commodity prices (tying them to some price index, such as that for the imports of the developing countries) is not mentioned explicitly in the resolution, but the UNCTAD IV discussions occurred in the context of considerable debates about the pros and cons of indexation. Of course indexation is only a special case of changing the secular trend in the relevant deflated price to a value of zero.

Why is there this interest in increasing the secular trend of commodity prices? As is indicated in Section 1.3, there is a fairly wide consensus that greater access to foreign exchange, *ceteris paribus*, raises the probability of increasing the economic welfare of developing countries. If the secular trend of commodity export prices can be altered by commodity agreements or by other policies, the revenue generated by such exports can be changed. The revenue changes in the same direction as the price change if the relevant price elasticity of demand is less than one.

What happens to the secular trend of deflated commodity prices has been a subject of considerable controversy in the development literature. The classical economists believed that the terms of trade would shift in favor of the primary commodities because of diminishing returns to fixed natural resources. Prebisch argues that these trends are inevitably downward because of lower income elasticities for these products, the concentration of market power in the developed nations, and natural-resource-saving biases in technological progress.

Empirical explorations have come up with estimates of positive, negative, and no secular trends, depending on the time period explored and the definitions used.

The sensitivity to the time period used should be clear if you look at Fig. 4.1 again. For the whole 1954-1975 period, the secular trend is negative, as is indicated by the dashed line. But what if one looks only at 1961-1974? Then the secular tendency probably is positive. How then can one avoid distortions in the estimates of the secular tendencies due to the particular choice of years for the estimates? The answer is to choose a reasonably long period and to have both endpoints of the period be at about the same point on the cycle (that is, both at peaks or both at troughs—but not from trough to peak as in the 1961-1974 example, nor vice versa).

The problem with definitions has several aspects. For example, there is the question of how to treat quality changes. To calculate movements in the terms of trade we would like to compare prices of products that are unchanging over time (for example, the price of a pound of Ghanaian cocoa in the New York spot commodity market relative to the price of number-one-grade hard winter wheat in the same market). Otherwise there is a problem of distinguishing between price changes for the same quality and quality changes. Consider, for example, the problems in conducting a price index for television sets or automobiles of a constant quality in the postwar period, given the very substantial quality changes experienced. In calculating the terms of trade of primary commodity exporters over time, the numerator generally is not a large problem in regard to quality changes. It is the price of some well-specified commodity that probably has remained homogeneous over time. The denominator, however, represents the market basket of goods that the developing countries import. These are primarily manufactured or processed products from the developed nations for which quality changes have occurred rapidly in many cases. The statistical offices for the develped countries do attempt to adjust for quality changes, but there is some independent evidence that they do not correct sufficiently for such changes. To the extent that there is such an underadjustment, the price indices used in the denominator overstate inflation, and, therefore, the ratio overstates the deterioration in the terms of trade.

A second example is the question of how to treat changes in transportation costs. The comparisons between the price of Ghanaian cocoa (or of some other relevant primary commodity) in the New York market and the export price index of the developed countries, for example, may overstate deteriorations in the terms of trade for primary commodities if transportation costs have declined (and vice versa). This is so because the developing country is not interested in relative prices in the developed nations, but in relative prices at its own ports. The relation between the two is as follows:

$$\frac{PA^{LDC}}{PM^{LDC}} = \frac{PA^{DC} - TCA}{PM^{DC} + TCM}$$

where A is the primary export of the developing country,
  M is the manufactured import of the developing country,
  PA is the price of A,
  PM is the price of M,
  TCA is the transportation cost for a unit of A,
  TCM is the transportation cost for a unit of M,
  LDC refers to the less developed or developing country, and
  DC refers to the developed country.

The reader should be able to see that the terms of trade relevant to the developing country increase more (or deteriorate less) than the price ratio in the developed countries indicates if transportation costs fall. For most of the postwar period (although possibly not since 1973), transportation costs have tended to decline. Therefore, commonly used ratios of the terms of trade of developing countries probably tend to understate increases (or overstate decreases) in the terms of trade actually relevant to the developing countries.

There are still other questions about the appropriate definition of the terms of trade. Is the simple export-price-to-import-price ratio really of most interest, or is it some other related concept? International economists have devised a series of alternative measures in hopes of better representing the purchasing power of the primary exports or of the inputs used to produce them. We do not explore these alternatives here. The interested reader is referred to any international economics textbook. Instead we focus on the ratio of the price of the commodity of interest to an index representing price movements in the developed countries that are the major source of imports for the developing nations. We use this definition of the terms of trade for primary commodities (or, equivalently, the deflated or real commodity price) because of its simplicity and because it is most widely used.

Fig. 4.1 indicates the secular trend for the primary product terms of trade for thirty-four leading nonpetroleum commodity exports of the developing world for the years 1950-1975. This time period begins right before the Korean War commodity boom and ends right after the commodity boom of 1973-1974, so it does not seem to be particularly biased. The estimated exponential growth rate in the secular tendency is −0.98 percent, which implies a decline of about 20 percent over the 1954-1975 period. In the aggregate over the past quarter century, therefore, the developing country primary commodity exporters do appear to have experienced a secular deterioration in their terms of trade, although the reader should keep in mind the qualifications made above in regard to possible biases due to changes in quality and in transportation costs. Any particular decline in relative prices is not good or bad, nor just or unjust in itself. However, this particular decline tended to increase world economic inequality, which in the present author's value system is unfortunate.

As is the case for fluctuations, the aggregate measure of the secular tendency in the primary terms of trade tends to conceal some diverse patterns for individual commodities. Therefore, let us turn to consideration of the secular tendencies in the movements of the deflated prices for individual commodities.

The first three columns of Table 4.1 give the average annual growth rates of market prices, values, and deflated values for the ten core and seven other UNCTAD commodities over the 1953-1972 period. This time period includes neither the Korean War boom, which peaked in 1951, nor the main part of the 1973-1974 boom. The first column in Table 4.2 presents estimates of the secular trends in the deflated prices for the same commodities plus fifteen others for the 1950-1975 years. This time period is identical to the one used in Fig. 4.1, with the Korean War peak near the beginning and the 1973-1974 boom near the end. Therefore, it is not obvious that either set of estimates is terribly biased due to the beginning and terminal dates of the

Table 4.2 Secular trends in deflated prices for UNCTAD core commodities, UNCTAD other commodities, and additional commodities of possible interest, 1950-1975*

1. Core commodities	(1)			
Coffee	− .035		Iron Ore	− .017
Cocoa	− .024		Maize	.029
Tea	− .030		Tobacco	− .015
Sugar	− .004§		Lumber	− .008
Cotton	− .038		Hides and skins	− .030
Rubber	− .058		Groundnut oil	− .033
Jute	− .018		Olive oil	− .010§
Sisal†	− .004§		Coconut oil	− .023
Copper	.004§		Palm oil	− .028
Tin	.004§		Linseed oil	− .035
			Animal fats and oils‡	− .030
2. Other commodities			Soybean oil‡	− .015§
			Cottonseed oil‡	− .016
Wheat	− .021		Palm kernel oil‡	− .006§
Rice	− .008§		Lead	− .028
Bananas	− .037			
Beef and veal	.026			
Wool	− .041			
Bauxite	.019			

*Calculated from UNCTAD price indices in United Nations [7] and OECD GDP price deflator.

†1954-1975

‡1954-1974

§Not significantly different from zero at standard 5 percent level.

time periods.[6] Possible problems due to variations in quality and in transportation costs remain.

Despite the differences in the sample periods and the use of somewhat different data, these two tables point to the same general conclusions.

1. The secular trends in these commodity prices have tended to be negative in these periods. In Table 4.2 significantly negative estimates are indicated for six of the ten core commodities, ten of the seventeen UNCTAD com-

---

6 The estimates for rubber, sisal, palm kernel oil, soybean oil, and cottonseed oil in Table 4.2 are based on a shorter 1954-1974/5 period. Therefore, they may be biased upwards.

modities, and twenty-one of the thirty-two total commodities. Significantly positive estimates are indicated for none of the core commodities, two of the seventeen UNCTAD commodities, and two of the thirty-two total commodities. For the rest the trends are not significantly nonzero.[7]

2. The trends tend to be positive or not significantly nonzero more for minerals than for others. However, the tendency is weak. For example, the strongest positive trend is for beef and veal, and the estimates for lead and iron ore are significantly negative.

3. There is no correlation between the degree of price instability (Section 4.1) and the magnitude of the secular price trends for the seventeen UNCTAD commodities.

4. Likewise, there is not much evidence of a positive association between income elasticities (column 4 in Table 5.1) and the secular price trends. This observation is somewhat surprising because income grew substantially in the period of interest, thus causing the demand curves to shift out in the price-quantity plane to degrees that depend on the income elasticity of demand. Everything else being equal, the price increases should be greater the higher the income elasticities. Apparently, other factors, such as differential supply shifts and differential supply price elasticities, swamp this tendency.

5. The rates of growth of deflated values tend to be correlated with the rates of growth of prices for the seventeen UNCTAD commodities (columns 1 and 3 in Table 4.1). However, in five cases, quantity changes were sufficiently large that the signs of the mean growth rate of price and of deflated value are opposite (for example, cocoa, jute, rice, bananas, and iron ore).

4.3 HISTORICAL EXPERIENCE WITH INTERNATIONAL COMMODITY AGREEMENTS AND CARTELS

We have considered the historical experience in regard to fluctuations and secular trends for deflated prices in international primary commodity markets. We now turn to historical attempts to regulate the markets by international commodity agreements or producer cartels.

Attempts to control international commodity markets have been many throughout the twentieth century. The number of substantive efforts is well over fifty. To this end conferences of coffee and sugar producers were held as early as 1902, and the Brazil coffee "valorization scheme" was instituted in 1907. Before World War I, however, such schemes generally were considered uneconomic and impractical.

---

7 "Significantly" is used in this discussion to mean probably not zero in a statistical sense. For further discussion of how such estimates are obtained, see Appendix B.

The experience of World War I made controls seem more necessary because of the severe dislocation in markets during and after the war, and more practical because of the wartime expansion of governments into many other activities that previously had been considered unwarranted market interferences and virtually impossible administratively. Control attempts in copper, tin, rubber, and coffee in the early postwar years were followed by a number of other efforts for wheat, beef, wool, tea, timber, and camphor. Generalizations about these efforts are almost impossible, except to note that there was no coordination among them and that all were dominated by producers.

The shock of the Great Depression caused a collapse of all existing control programs by the early 1930s. The resulting substantial excess capacity then caused producers to become very interested in reestablishing, extending, and creating international commodity control programs, such as for cotton, tin, and tea. These efforts continued on an individual commodity basis, but discussions on a broader multicommodity basis occurred at League of Nations conferences on problems of raw materials in 1921, 1927, and 1937 and at the London Monetary and Economic Conference in 1935. Such discussions tended to have a cautionary tone, to worry about possible permanent market interference, and to weigh substantially consumer interests.

World War II caused a strengthening of demand. Military and political considerations took precedence over commodity trade agreements with a pure economic basis. Most such agreements ceased to function or were suspended until the end of the war. Early in the war the Mutal Aid Agreement and the Atlantic Charter, while not focusing explicitly on commodities, stressed the elimination of trade barriers and trade discrimination and emphasized commercial agreements in harmony with expanded production and trade. The basic motive for the next round of international conferences was the implementation of these goals. The United Nations Conference on Food and Agriculture in 1943 began an extensive examination of international commodity problems, which was to culminate in efforts to establish an International Trade Organization at the Havana Conference in 1947. In between, a new wave of commodity studies and proposals was induced. In part because of their dominance on the demand side, the United States and the United Kingdom were instrumental in the discussions. The general principles enunciated included the use of international commodity agreements to promote the expansion of an orderly world economy by price stabilization without distorting the secular trends. Consumers were to be represented effectively with an equal vote in such agreements. Corrective adjustments were to be encouraged in the production of commodities for which a surplus existed. Output restrictions were to be avoided except transitorily in extreme cases. The Havana Conference, although unsuccessful in establishing an International Trade Organization, did codify this set of principles in Chapter 6 of the Havana Charter. In 1947 the United Nations Economic and Social Council adopted the principles embodied in the Havana Charter and recommended their use in all new commodity agreements.

In the immediate postwar period, pent-up demands led to considerable shortages in some commodities and a revival of interest in international commodity agreements, largely from the consumer side. Study groups were established for cotton in 1945, wool in 1946, and tin, sugar, and rubber in 1947, and the tea agreement was again in force. In the late 1940s, threats of emerging surpluses appeared and study-group effort intensified due to strong producer interests. In 1949 the International Wheat Agreement was signed. Another sharp shift occurred in the early 1950s with the Korean War boom. In 1951 prices hit peak levels for a number of commodities. The major importers started pressure for controls to ensure price stability and proposed study groups for a large number of commodities. These interests faded as the Korean conflict drew to an end and supplies increased. The abnormal demands in the early 1950s led to overexpansion in some commodities and renewed interest in some form of commodity controls by producers. Wheat and tea agreements remained in force, a sugar agreement was initiated in 1953, and a tea agreement came in 1956. In the late 1950s the Latin American coffee producers cooperated in a cartel that laid the foundations for the International Coffee Agreement of 1963. At about the same time the United States-Cuban-Union of Soviet Socialist Republic problems led to the demise of the sugar agreement.

In the early 1950s many of the developing countries were focusing on import substitution as a means to resolve problems with foreign exchange shortages. With the substantial and widespread decline in international commodity prices, renewed interest appeared among the developing countries in the possibility of using international commodity agreements to alleviate a range of problems, but especially the perceived deterioration in their terms of trade. Over the same period the United Nations' position on commodity agreements moved from its apparent immediate positive agreement with the conservative principles enunciated in the Havana Charter to evermore enthusiastic support of the use of commodity agreements on a broader basis with fewer constraints to rectify more problems.

The establishment of UNCTAD in the early 1960s reflected this new viewpoint. In 1964, 1968, and 1972, UNCTAD I, II, and III all placed considerable emphasis on improving the operation of international commodity markets from the point of view of the developing nations. UNCTAD, which has taken a major role in promoting study groups for international commodity agreements, throughout the 1960s provided strong support for a cocoa agreement that culminated in a pact in 1970 that was renewed in 1975. Other recent activities generally encouraged by UNCTAD include the reestablishment of a limited sugar agreement in 1968, the transformation of the wheat agreement into the International Grains Agreement in 1967, and then the reversal to wheat alone in 1971, and the establishment of agreements for tea in 1969 and for cocoa, sisal and henequen in 1970. Counter to the trend for more commodity agreements was the effective demise of the International Coffee Agreement in 1972, but a new agreement was negotiated at the end of 1975.

In addition to such international commodity agreements, international producer cartels also have been formed in recent years. Of course, the most well known of these is the Organization of Petroleum Exporting Countries, or OPEC, which succeeded in raising oil prices by over 400 percent in 1973-1974. There are claims that the International Bauxite Association has had similar success and demonstrates that "oil was not unique." Other producer associations that recently have been active include Cafe Mondial, the Intergovernmental Council of Copper-Exporting Countries (CIPEC), the Association of Natural Rubber Producing Countries, the Union of Banana Exporting Countries (UBEC), and the Association of Iron Ore Exporting Countries. At least the first three of these took some measures to limit supplies after the price downturn of 1974.

This brief survey brings us up to the period immediately before UNCTAD IV, which was discussed in Section 2.2. It indicates a cyclical interest in international commodity agreements, with consuming nations more interested for reasons of price stability when prices are high and producing nations (especially in the developing world) more interested in increasing prices when downward movements are current. The cyclical fluctuations probably are around a secular trend of increasing interest in controlling commodity markets, especially among developing nations and in the United States.

What does this past experience tell us about the success of efforts to control international commodity markets? One way to answer this question is to use the survival test. This approach has the advantage of avoiding the need to have data on the success in attaining specific objectives. Presumably, organizations that survive must be satisfying their objectives at least minimally. For the fifty-one international commodity cartels for which Eckbo [8] could find sufficient data to include in his sample, the average duration of the formal agreements was 5.4 years (4.3 years if one outlier is excluded) and the median was 2.5 years.[8] By this test, it would seem fair to conclude that the majority of the efforts in this sample were not very successful.

---

8 That is, there were twenty-five cases that lasted less than 2.5 years and twenty-five cases that lasted more than 2.5 years.

Although information is quite scarce, we can go somewhat further in commenting on the success of past efforts in terms of the two specific objectives that are emphasized in the UNCTAD IV resolution (see Section 2.2) and one or the other of which has been the focus of most attempts to control commodity markets.

First, consider the question of price stabilization. Law [9] finds most past experiences that he reviews to have been inadequate in attaining this objective. For coffee, the average annual price fluctuation was at least 50 percent greater during the agreement years of 1964-1972 than for the preceding nonagreement period of 1950-1963. For sugar, the average annual price fluctuation was at least 75 percent greater for the twelve recent years of control than during the eleven other noncontrol years (if the years dominated by the United States-Cuban confrontation are eliminated). For rubber, the international agreements were price destabilizing. For cocoa, the 1970 agreement has failed to come into effect because of prices high above the maximum posited in the agreement. Only for wheat and tea did price stability apparently increase during the tenure of international agreements, and in those cases much more because of United States and Canadian production and stockpiling decisions that were made outside of the agreements.

Smith and Schink [10] much more extensively assess the International Tin Agreement, which is the longest ongoing agreement and which generally has been regarded as a qualified, but respectable, success with a primary objective of stabilization. Their approach is to simulate developments in the world tin market with and without the international tin agreement and with and without United States stockpile activities using an econometric model of the international tin market.[9] They have four basic conclusions: (1) The Tin Agreement only marginally stabilized prices and producer incomes. The United States stockpile transactions, conducted outside of the agreement, were of far greater importance. (2) The Tin Agreement endured in part because the existence of the United States strategic stockpile deprived it of the power to make the critical price decisions that otherwise would have intensified producer-consumer conflicts.[10] (3) If the Tin Agreement had been designed as an effective price stabilizer along lines suggested for other commodities, it probably would have fallen apart. (4) Meaningful reductions in price fluctuations for more volatile products may require far larger buffer stocks than had previously been suggested.[11]

---

9 This approach is adopted in Chapters 5 and 6. See those chapters for more details and for necessary qualifications.

10 Note that this argument casts doubt on the survival test as a measure of minimal success.

11 We return to this question in Chapter 5.

The available evidence, therefore, does not seem to be very positive in regard to the success of past international commodity agreements in stabilizing prices. Of course, in some cases price stabilization was, at most, a secondary objective. Let us now turn to the second (and perhaps the dominant) major goal in the UNCTAD IV resolution: increasing the prices (and therefore the export earnings) of the affected commodities.

Some of the numerous attempts to control international commodity markets clearly have been successful in increasing prices, at least in the short run. The Stevenson Plan of restricting output and exports of natural rubber in the 1920s apparently raised prices significantly for several years, although partly at the long-run cost of inducing more research on synthetic substitutes. The recent coffee agreements are estimated to have transferred resources from consumers to producers at the rate of $500 to $600 million per year. Eckbo reports that nineteen of the fifty-one cartels for which he was able to get systematic data succeeded in temporarily raising prices at least 200 percent above the unit cost of production and distribution. OPEC and IBA are current examples for oil and bauxite, respectively.

But there are an even larger number of unsuccessful attempts to increase prices substantially. Moreover, while the successful attempts seem to survive longer than the unsuccessful ones, they still do not seem to last very long. Among successful efforts in Eckbo's sample, the median duration is only 4 years and the average is only 6.6 years.[12] Why are so many efforts unsuccessful and why do the successes not last longer?

A number of theoretical and piecemeal empirical efforts have been made to answer these questions. They are the basis for the characteristics favorable to oligopolist price collusion that were given in Section 3.4.

However, the only attempt to answer these questions by examining the quantitative experience of a large number of attempts to organize international commodity markets is the study by Eckbo of fifty-one such efforts, to which reference has already been made several times. In this attempt, the crude data available force simple categorizations and preclude sophisticated statistical analysis. Nevertheless, some patterns seem to be clear. Successful efforts to raise international commodity prices tended substantially to be associated with higher concentration of production, higher concentration of foreign trade, higher price elasticities of demand,[13] higher income elasticities of demand, less possibilities of short-term substitution,[14] a higher share

---

12 This mean excludes one outlier (sixty-one years for iodine). If the outlier is included, the mean increases to 9.5 years.

13 This result is surprising, and does not seem consistent with the claim of less short-run substitution possibilities.

14 But success tended to be associated with higher long-term substitution possibilities.

of foreign trade controlled by members of the agreement,[15] low cost differences among producers in the agreement, and less government involvement. The successful efforts seemed to be sustained longer in cases in which concentration of production was high, demand was price inelastic, the members' market share was high, the members had cost advantages over outsiders, and governments were not involved in operations. Successful agreements broke down most often due to competition among the members,[16] with competition from nonmembers being the second most common cause.

What are the implications of the historical experience for current proposals for commodity agreements, such as the UNCTAD resolution? They seem to be mixed. Past efforts at price stabilization generally have not been very successful. Past efforts at increasing prices have been successful in a number of cases in the short run, with substantial gains to producers that probably outweighed the longer-run costs due to the induced expanded production from fringe producers and the induced development of new substitutes. The repetition of such experiences possibly would be of considerable benefit to current producers. However, many of the commodity markets on which UNCTAD is concentrating do not have many of the characteristics that in the past have been associated with short-run successes of producers' cartels (see Section 3.4). In these cases, therefore, even short-run market regulation may have a reasonable probability of success only if the consuming nations can be persuaded to join in the effort, as UNCTAD proposes.

But the past is not a complete guide to the future. In the late 1970s the developing producer nations may be more cohesive than in the past because of the examples of OPEC and IBA, their growing power and latitude of movement in an increasingly pluralistic world with some form of détente instead of Cold War bipolarism,[17] and their common perceived need for a new economic order. The developed consuming nations may be more accommodating because of the same factors and the growing perception that access to primary commodity supplies and moderating inflation are important considerations for their own self-interests. The result may well be a

---

15 But the members' share of total production did not tend to be associated with success.

16 The OPEC strategy of leaving the decision concerning the allocation of the cartel shares among its member substantially to the oil companies may lessen intra-OPEC disputes and prolong its existence.

17 The judgment that their political power is growing is not incontestable. Perhaps the developing nations had more political power in an important sense while they could bargain with the superpowers within the framework of the more intense Cold War confrontation. In some cases even in the earlier colonial period, producers of some commodities may have had more power relative to consumers since they then were represented by the relatively strong colonial powers (which also, of course, represented the consumer interests).

higher probability of at least short- or medium-run success for the UNCTAD-type proposal than past experience alone might suggest.

4.4 CONCLUSIONS

In this chapter we have reviewed the historical experience in international commodity markets in regard to price fluctuations, price trends, and previous commodity agreements and producers' cartels.

One major objective of many international commodity agreements and of the UNCTAD proposal is to limit price fluctuations. Motives for this objective include limiting the inducements for the development of synthetic substitutes, lessening disruptive effects on planning of foreign exchange fluctuations, and increasing the cooperation of consuming nations in schemes that increase the revenues producers receive.

The UNCTAD ten core commodities have experienced relatively great price fluctuations in recent decades. For seven of the ten the average price fluctuations from the trend have exceeded 10 percent, and for three they have exceeded 20 percent. Fluctuations of such magnitude indeed may have some of the adverse effects indicated in the previous paragraph. Such fluctuations seem to have been greater for commodities with lower price elasticities and lesser for those with a highly vertically integrated market structure, as economic theory suggests. These price fluctuations have been associated with relatively large revenue fluctuations for most of the core commodities, although for half of them the revenue fluctuations are smaller than are those for prices because of compensating movements in quantities. Finally, such fluctuations do seem to have been relatively large for the developing countries in comparison to developed ones, especially in the 1970s.

A second major objective of many international commodity agreements and of the UNCTAD proposal is to increase the secular trend in the terms of trade of the developing countries primary commodity producers in order to increase their command over foreign exchange. After noting a number of qualifications that are needed in considering this question, we have come to the qualified conclusion that the terms of trade of the primary commodities of interest to the developing countries did tend to decline in the 1950-1975 quarter century, although less so for the minerals than for most others.

After examining the historical fluctuations and the secular trends in international commodity prices, we have reviewed the historical experience of international commodity agreements and producer cartels. Interest in such arrangements seems to have increased secularly in the twentieth century, but with substantial fluctuations. When commodity prices have been high, consumers have been more interested. When commodity prices have been low, producers have been more interested.

Such arrangements have not been very successful in stabilizing prices. However, almost 40 percent of the fifty-one cases for which systematic data are available have succeeded in temporarily raising prices at least 200 percent above the unit cost of production and distribution. These more successful efforts were characterized by higher concentration of foreign trade, higher income elasticities of demand, less possibilities of short-term substitution, a higher share of foreign trade controlled by members of the agreement, and low cost differentials among members of the agreement—all of which seem to be reasonable.[18] The successful efforts were sustained longer in cases in which concentration of production was high, demand was price inelastic, the market share of members was high, and the members had cost advantages over outsiders—once again, a reasonable set of characteristics.[19] Successful agreements broke down most often due to competition among members, with competition from nonmembers being next most important. Their average duration was 6.6 years (excluding one outlier).

The implications of this experience for current proposed commodity agreements, such as the UNCTAD resolution, are mixed. The repetition of the past experience in increasing prices for six or seven years probably would result in short-run benefits to developing country producers that would outweigh the longer-run costs of inducing expanded competition from synthetics and from fringe producers. However, the commodities of interest are not particularly distinguished by the characteristics that have led to even short-term success for producers' cartels in the past. Therefore, even short-run market regulation may have a reasonable probability of success only if the consumer nations can be persuaded to cooperate in order to enforce discipline. The growing strength and cohesion of the developing nations and the more accommodating posture of the developed nations probably lead to a higher probability of at least short-run success for an UNCTAD-type proposal than past experience alone might suggest.

REFERENCES

1. R. D. Hansen, et. al. *The U. S. and World Development: Agenda for Action, 1976.* New York: published for Overseas Development Council by Praeger, 1976.

2. UNCTAD. "An Integrated Commodity Program." Geneva: UNCTAD, 1976.

3. J. R. Behrman. *The New International Economic Order: Commodity Agreements.* Washington: Overseas Development Council, 1977.

4. UNCTAD. "Progress Report on Storage Costs and Warehouse Facilities." Geneva: UNCTAD, 1975.

---

18 They also were characterized by less government involvement and by higher price elasticities of demand, the latter of which is surprising and may not be consistent with less possibilities of short-term substitution.

19 Once again, less government involvement also seemed associated with longer success.

5. UNCTAD. "A Common Fund for the Financing of Commodity Stocks: Amounts, Terms and Prospective Sources of Finances," Geneva: UNCTAD, 1975.

6. UNCTAD. "Resolution Adopted by the Conference: Integrated Program for Commodities." Geneva: UNCTAD, 1976.

7. United Nations. *Monthly Bulletin of Statistics*. 1958-1976.

8. P. L. Eckbo. "OPEC and the Experience of Previous International Commodity Cartels." Cambridge, Mass.: M. I. T. Energy Laboratory Working Paper, 1975.

9. A. D. Law. *International Commodity Agreements: Setting, Performance, and Prospects*. Lexington, Mass.: Lexington Books, 1975.

10. G. W. Smith and G. R. Schink. "The International Tin Agreement: A Reassessment." Houston, Texas: Rice University, Program of Development Studies Discussion Paper No. 69, 1975.

Simulations of   5
Proposed International
Commodity
Agreements: General
Characteristics

In the previous two chapters we have considered what economic theory and the examination of history can tell us about the functioning of international commodity markets and the possible impact of proposed international commodity agreements, such as the UNCTAD integrated commodity program. Both of these modes of analysis have given us useful insights, but both have definite limitations. Theory, for example, can take us only so far without specific assumptions about the shapes of the underlying supply and demand curves.

Now we proceed to extend our analysis by simulating what would happen if proposed international commodity agreements were implemented. To do so, in an important sense we combine theory with the historical data. We use theory to specify a model of each international commodity market. Then we use historical data to estimate the parameters or coefficients in the models. Finally we use the estimated models to simulate what would happen if international commodity agreements such as UNCTAD has proposed were in effect.

Section 5.1 presents the major methodological steps in the simulation mode of analysis. Section 5.2 discusses the assumptions that underlie the simulations. Section 5.3 considers the first major aim of most commodity agreements and of the UNCTAD proposal: the stabilization of commodity prices around the historical trends. Section 5.4 investigates the second major goal: increasing the secular real price trends. Section 5.5 gives conclusions.

5.1 METHODOLOGICAL STEPS IN SIMULATION ANALYSIS[1]

This section considers the basic methodological steps in the simulation process. The specific examples used are related to international commodity

---

1 Appendix B examines the methodology in more detail.

markets, but the same general process could be used to investigate a wide range of economic, social, and political problems and policies. Each of three major steps are considered in turn: model specification, model estimation, and model simulation.

5.1.1 Model Specification

The first step is the specification of a model of the process under examination. A model simplifies and abstracts from reality in order to focus on the essentials of the phenomenon of interest. This abstraction helps us to understand better the phenomenon and to predict what would happen if certain changes occurred. A model usually is the representation of some theoretical analysis of the situation.

One sometimes hears the expression: "That may be all right in theory, but not in practice." What does that mean in our context? Apparently it means that that particular theory does not capture the essence of the situation given the interests of the observer. That is, that particular theory is not a good theory for the purpose of analyzing the problem of concern. What is needed is a good theory—one that does capture the essential elements of the phenomenon. What the commentator should distinguish between is not "theory versus practice," but "good theory versus bad theory" for the question of interest.

The model we use for our analysis of international commodity markets is that suggested by the theory of pure competition. Section 3.3 and Appendix A discuss this model in some detail. We choose this model because we consider it a good approximation to reality for most of the initial producers and final consumers (perhaps in processed form) of the majority of the UNCTAD core commodities. At the start and the end of the production-to-consumption chain, these individuals or entities do not appear to be able to affect market prices perceptibly, which is the essential condition for pure competition to hold. To the extent that there are exceptions in the form of large participants in the market in the middle of the chain (and perhaps at the beginning for the minerals) in the form of large firms or government organizations, we are assuming that the existence of limit pricing due to possible new entrants or substitutes results in approximately competitive behavior (see Section 3.4).

In essence, our model for each commodity consists of four components: a supply relation, a demand for current use relation, a price inventory relation, and a market-clearing condition.[2] Thus we are collapsing the various

---

2 In our empirical estimation of the supply and demand relations we divide the total world into three regions because we think that the parameters and lag structures may differ among the developing, developed, and centrally planned groups. On a general level, however, the theory is the same for each country group.

stages of supply and demand into one relation on each side so that the international market can be represented as in Fig. 5.1. We consider each of the basic relations in turn.

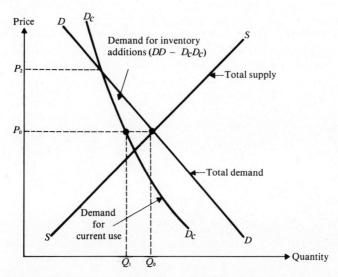

Fig. 5.1 Supply, demand for current use, and demand for inventory changes in model of international commodity market

Before turning to these relations, however, let us reiterate some of the lessons of Chapter 3. By assuming the existence of purely competitive-like behavior, we are assuming that each of the participating entities on the supply and demand side of the market acts as if it cannot perceptibly affect market prices. We are *not* making any assumptions about the desirability of such a market system. Any particular social welfare function is *not* being maximized unless there are no externalities, there is no risk aversion, and the distribution of input ownership is just right—which is *very* improbable. Moreover, purely competitive-like behavior in these individual commodity markets does not even imply efficiency, given the existence of externalities, risk aversion, and nonmarginal cost pricing in the rest of the world. In summary, we are interested here in the purely competitive model only because of its ability to predict behavior (in other words, "positive economics"), not because there is necessarily anything desirable about that behavior (in other words, "normative economics").

Now let us consider briefly each of the four relations in our model of international commodity agreements.[3]

---

3 Appendix B provides much more detail for interested readers.

1. Supply. Producers are assumed to decide what to supply on the basis of the product prices they expect to prevail at the end of the production process (harvest time, for agricultural commodities), the input prices they face, and the production technology they know. At higher expected product prices, everything else being equal, planned production will be higher, so the supply curve (*SS*) is upward sloping in Fig. 5.1. Actual production depends on the decisions taken by the producers and on factors beyond their control, such as the weather. Lagged values of variables are used to represent adjustment processes and the creation of price expectations on the bases of past and current prices.

2. Demand for current use. Consumers are assumed to decide what quantity of a commodity to consume on the basis of their income in constant dollars, the price of that commodity relative to prices for other goods, changes in tastes or technology, and other less important variables that cannot easily be represented explicitly. At higher prices for the commodity, everything else being equal, the quantity demand will be less, so the demand for current consumption curve (D_cD_c) in Fig. 5.1 is downward sloping. Once again, lagged values are used to represent adjustment and expectation creation processes.

3. Private inventories. In addition to the demand for current use, there is a demand for net additions or withdrawals from private inventories. Desired levels of private inventories reflect transaction and seasonal demands to ensure inputs for normal operations, precautionary demands in case of a supply disruption due to bad weather or some similar event, and speculative demands related to expectations about future price movements. The basic determinants of the demand for desired inventory changes include the expected level of the activity in which the commodity is used (for example, chocolate production, and so on for cocoa beans), the storage and interest cost of holding inventories, the current and expected prices of the commodity, and other less important variables that cannot easily be represented explicitly. The demand for desired inventory additions ($DD - D_cD_c$ in Fig. 5.1) will be less as the current price becomes higher, everything else (including expected future prices) being equal. Note that at high enough current prices (above P_2 in Fig. 5.1), desired inventories will be reduced instead of increased. Adjustment and expectational processes once more are represented by lagged variables.

4. Market-clearing relation. Total world production goes to current consumption or to private inventories. In equilibrium, there are adjustments in the market price so that total production just equals desired current consumption and desired inventories. In Fig. 5.1, the price P_0 is such an equilibrium point. At this price supply is Q_0, demand for current use is Q_1, and the demand for inventory additions is $Q_1 - Q_0$—so total supply just equals total demand. At any higher price, total supply exceeds total demand, so there is undesired inventory accumulation and pressure for the price to fall. At any lower price, total demand exceeds total supply, so there is undesired inventory decumulation and pressure for the price to rise.

The complete model. These four relations comprise the complete model of an international commodity market. This model determines four endogenous variables: production or supply, demand for current use, demand for inventory change, and the price of the commodity. The exact values of these variables depend on the shape and location of the curves in Fig. 5.1. In turn, these curves depend on the elasticities of supply and demand and on changes in exogenous variables, such as weather, income, other prices, and the costs of holding inventories. Figs. 5.2a and b illustrate the effects of good and bad weather in shifting the supply curve and of high and low income in shifting the demand curve. Starting from an initial equilibrium, such as the price P_0 in Fig. 5.1, such a shift will alter the solution values of all four endogenous variables.

For example, a shift to the left in the supply curve due to bad weather reduces the quantity supplied at each price. At the original equilibrium price of P_0 there are insufficient supplies to satisfy total demands, so unintended inventory decumulation occurs. This causes the price to rise, which results in a reduction in the quantity demanded along the total demand curve (*DD*). The price continues to increase until a new equilibrium is reached at which the quantity supplied on the leftward-shifted supply curve just equals the total desired demand. This adjustment process is complicated, however, because of the feedback of the changing price on the quantities supplied and demanded and because of the time required to adjust to the new situation. For this reason, explicit modeling, with elasticities and adjustment lags estimated from historical experience, is extremely useful in helping us understand what would happen in a commodity market if some change were introduced.

5.1.2 Estimation of the Model

The second step is to estimate the elasticities and the lagged patterns of adjustments in the relations of the model. Such estimates should be based on the best information available. In general this means that considerable weight should be placed on the historical data about events in the commodity market of interest. But this may not be such an easy process. The historical data reflect the complicated feedback and adjustment processes that are described in the previous paragraphs. To disentangle these we use standard statistical techniques to select estimates of the elasticities and of the adjustment lags in the model of the previous subsection that are most consistent

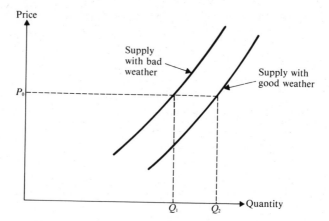

a) Shift in supply function due to change in weather

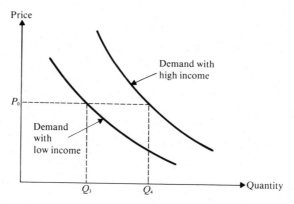

b) Shift in demand function due to change in per capita income

Figure 5.2

with the historical experience. Table 5.1 gives the estimated price elasticities of supply and price and income elasticities of demand for the UNCTAD core and other commodities. Note that these estimates indicate fairly limited price responses, especially in the short run, for most of these commodities. As was discussed in Section 3.3, low price elasticities mean that producers may gain from increased revenues and less variability in these revenues if price stabilization is introduced in a situation in which supply shifts dominate.

5.1.3 Simulations with the Models

The third step is to simulate the models. In a simulation the values of the endogenous variables in the model—supply, demand for current use, current additions to inventories, and the world price—are solved given the theoretical structure posited in Subsection 5.1.1, the estimated parameters and lag patterns obtained as described in Subsection 5.1.2, lagged values of endogenous variables to the extent they enter into the relations, and the values of all exogenous variables (including lags if necessary)—the deflator for the developed economies, income or gross national production and population in all of the consuming regions, the weather variables in the supplying regions, and the secular trends. Changing any one of these "givens" generally alters the values of all of the endogenous variables, although perhaps with lags.

The difficulty of solving a model depends on several factors: size, the degree of simultaneity, the extent of nonlinearities, the number of lagged endogenous variables. Our models are not too complicated to solve, although they are simultaneous and include several lagged endogenous variables. For our solutions we use a large-scale electronic computer.

To understand better our simulation results, it is useful to distinguish between one-period versus dynamic simulations. A one-period simulation solves the model for each period, given values of lagged endogenous variables from some source outside of the model (for example, historical values). Such a procedure captures the simultaneous or current period interaction, but not the dynamic effects over time. A dynamic simulation uses the simulated values from earlier periods for the lagged endogenous variables. Thus it captures the pattern of responses in the endogenous variables over time to a change in any of the givens. We discuss only dynamic simulations in this study.

Given this background, let us now discuss how we use simulations. We proceed first by testing our models by simulating over the historical period with all exogenous variables taking on their actual values. We do this because at times the individual relations in a model may appear to be very reasonable and quite consistent with reality, but when solved together as a group lead to very strange results. In such a case it is necessary to go back and reexamine—and perhaps reestimate—the individual relations.

We then test the sensitivity of our models to changes in various exogenous variables. Do they respond reasonably to different levels of income, different types of weather, and so forth? If not, how should they be modified? Need relations in the model be reestimated?

After answering such questions and making any necessary modifications, we then simulate the impact of international commodity agreements.

5.2 ASSUMPTIONS OF THE SIMULATIONS

The strength of simulations is that they enable us to obtain estimates of the orders of magnitude associated with international commodity agreement operations on the basis of estimates of the market structure, including si-

Table 5.1 Summary of ordinary least squares regression estimates of short- and long-run price elasticities of supply and long-run demand elasticities with respect to price and income for seventeen UNCTAD commodities*

Commodity and country grouping	Price elasticity of supply		Demand elasticity with respect to:	
	Short-run	*Long-run*	*Price*	*Income*
1. Core commodities	(1)	(2)	(3)	(4)
Coffee				
Developed			− .2	.2
Developing	.0	.3	− .3	.4
Socialist			− 1.3	1.5
World	.0	.3		
Cocoa				
Developed			− .3	.0
Developing	.0	.3	− .1	1.4
Socialist			− .6	1.2
World	.0	.3		
Tea				
Developed	.0	.1	− .1	.0
Developing	.1	.2	− .1	.4
Socialist	.0	.7	− .5	.0
World				
Sugar				
Developed	.0	.2	− .0	.3
Developing	.0	.2	− .1	.8
Socialist	.0	.7	− .5	.4
World				
Cotton				
Developed	1.4	1.4	− .4	1.2
Developing	.1	.1	− .2	.5
Socialist	.0	1.0	− .1	.0
World				
Rubber				
Developed				
Developing	.0	.4		
Socialist				
World	.0	.4	− .5	1.0
Jute				
Developed				
Developing	.2	.2		
Socialist				
World	.2	.2	− .0	.0

*Short-run refers to responses in a year or less. Long-run refers to complete adjustment. Complete adjustment may take a number of years, e.g., the mean lag in supply price response is over eight years for coffee and cocoa and over six years for tea, bauxite, and copper. Lags on the demand side generally are shorter, but still mean lags of a year or two are not uncommon. More extended discussion of these estimates may be found in Adams and Behrman [1], Agosin [2], and Behrman [3].

Commodity and country grouping	Price elasticity of supply		Demand elasticity with respect to:	
	Short-run	Long-run	Price	Income
	(1)	(2)	(3)	(4)
Sisal				
Developed				
Developing	.1	.2		
Socialist				
World	.1	.2	– .0	.0
Copper				
Developed				
Developing				
Socialist				
World	.0	.1	– .4	1.0
Tin				
Developed				
Developing				
Socialist				
World	.0	.2	– 5.0	5.0
2. Other commodities				
Wheat				
Developed	.5	.4	– .5	.4
Developing	.0	.6	– .5	.0
Socialist	.0	1.0	.0	.2
World				
Rice				
Developed	.2	1.5	– .8	2.1
Developing	.0	.0	– .0	.0
Socialist	.0	.3	.0	.0
World				
Bananas				
Developed				
Developing				
Socialist				
World	.0	.0	– .5	.0
Beef & Veal				
Developed	.2	.8		
Developing	.0	.5		
Socialist	.0	.0		
World			– .2	
Wool				
Developed	.0	.0	– .3	1.8
Developing	.0	.5	– .2	1.1
Generally Planned	.0	.6	– .2	2.1
World				
Bauxite				
Developed				
Developing				
Socialist				
World	.0	.4	– 1.3	2.3
Iron Ore				
Developed				
Developing				
Socialist				
World	.0	.3	– .7	.0

multaneous feedbacks and critical lag patterns due to adjustment and expectational formation processes. This approach also has the advantage that all assumptions are explicit. Let us now list and discuss these assumptions in turn.

1. The models approximate well the structures of the markets despite the operations of the international commodity agreements. Some more explicit implications of this assumption are as follows: (a) Limit pricing (that is, pricing to deter too-rapid entry; see Section 3.4) and the threat of substitution in use continue to make aggregate supply and demand response relations sufficiently good approximations despite the existence of additional market power. (b) National policies that alter the relation between international and domestic prices (for example, marketing boards, export taxes, import taxes) continue to have the same effects as in the historical period from which data were obtained for the estimates. (c) Private inventory behavioral relations remain the same despite the existence of a buffer stock arrangement (see Assumption 3 below). (d) Elasticities and lags remain the same despite the reduction in price instability or possible changes in the secular price trends.

Some of these implications are quite strong. For example, private inventories might be expected to fall because of a reduction in speculation that prices could go above the ceiling level[4] (assuming that the buffer stock has sufficient commodity reserves) and the assurance of extra supplies from the buffer stock. On the other hand, there would also be a reduction in speculation that prices would go below the floor level (assuming that the buffer stock has sufficient financial reserves), which would tend to increase private inventories. Moreover, the reduction in risks of carrying inventories may cause them to rise, everything else being equal, if inventory holders are risk averse. The sensitivity of the simulations to structural changes in either direction for inventory behavior (or for any other aspect of the model) in principle could be explored through sensitivity analysis of the type that is mentioned at the end of this section.

2. Simulations over a recent particular historical period (1963-1972) provide useful information about likely orders of magnitude associated with the operation of buffer stock arrangements. The use of the decade starting in 1963 ties the results to the values of the exogenous variables in that particular period. However, that period is long enough to encompass a wide range of experience (for example, substantial fluctuations in the world economy). The length of the period, therefore, lessens the extent to which the total results are conditional on the particular choice of years, although the details of the time sequence obviously reflect that choice.

---

4 Speculation is further discussed under the third assumption below.

The use of a period as long as a decade is also useful because it permits coverage of enough years to encompass several commodity price cycles of historical duration. If, instead, a much shorter period were used, the results might be very sensitive to whether the start and end of the period happened to coincide with peaks or troughs in the price cycles. UNCTAD [4] gives the lengths of price cycles in the 1960-1974 period for nine of the ten UNCTAD core commodities (not including tea). Across all of these commodities the average is twenty-two months, with the averages for the individual commodities ranging from thirteen months for sugar to thirty-four months for coffee.[5] The maximum length ranges from twenty-six months for sugar to seventy-nine months for coffee, but for no other commodity is it greater than fifty-one months. A ten-year simulation period, therefore, should cover enough time for several price cycles of the duration historically experienced—although fewer for coffee than for the other commodities. It should be short enough, on the other hand, so that structural changes in the elasticities of the models due to reduced price fluctuations are not overwhelming. This is so since many of those changes relate to investment decisions with long gestation periods, and probably several years would be required before the stabilization was confidently viewed as sufficiently credible to induce large changes in investment.

3. The international commodity agreement is implemented by a buffer stock program, with no export or production quotas.[6] The buffer stock managers operate with sufficient financial reserves and sufficient commodity reserves so that they can buy or sell to keep the average annual deflated commodity price within a 15-percent band of a particular known secular real price trend for each commodity. The secular real price trend in the case of stabilization alone (Section 5.3) is that which prevailed for the quarter century starting in 1950 (see Table 3.2). In the case of stabilization around a higher secular trend than actually prevailed (Section 5.4), the trend used increases at an annual rate 2 percent greater than that experienced in 1950-1975.

---

5 The differential lengths of these cycles across commodities is interesting. To the extent that they originate in demand-side fluctuations, less differences across commodities might be expected since fluctuations in per capita income for the major demanders are highly synchronized across these commodities. To the extent that they originate in supply-side fluctuations, longer cycles might be expected for the commodities with longer gestation periods (that is, the tree crops and the minerals). Although the estimates for the shortest and longest average cycles (sugar and coffee) seem consistent with such a pattern, many of the others are not. For example, except for sugar, the shortest average cycles are for copper, cocoa, and rubber (a mineral and two tree crops)—and, except for coffee, the longest average cycle is for cotton.

6 Actual quotas and restrictions are used to the same extent as in the sample period, however, since the estimates of the parameters from historical data reflect the impact of any such policies.

If the deflated price otherwise would move to more than 15 percent below the target secular trend, the buffer stock purchases enough of the commodity to maintain this price floor. Buffer stock purchases reduce current supplies available for current demand and for private inventory additions. Therefore, they tend to increase the price, which has a feedback (perhaps with a lag) of inducing higher production and lower demand for current use. Because of the lags in the model, the effects of buffer stock actions taken in one year affect outcomes in subsequent years. For this reason the analysis of the time pattern of responses to the buffer stock action is somewhat complicated and dynamic simulations are required instead of one-period simulations (see Subsection 5.1.3). If the deflated price otherwise would go above the ceiling, which is 15 percent above the target secular real price trend, the buffer stock sells the commodity from its stocks, with the opposite results.

This assumption about the operation of the buffer stock has a number of subcomponents that merit some comments.

The existence of sufficient financial reserves means that the buffer stock can always buy to defend the price floor, which should discourage destabilizing speculation. The existence of sufficient commodity reserves to be able always to defend the price ceiling also should discourage destabilizing speculation. An example of the latter type of destabilizing speculation would be large purchases by speculators (which would tend to increase the price) under the assumption that the commodity could later be sold profitably at a real price above the ceiling band. The reasons for the assumption that the buffer stock can always maintain the desired price band are because it permits the simulation of the ongoing behavior of buffer stock stabilization without overemphasis on the end points of the scheme and because it avoids the difficult question of how speculators might behave. However, for some commodities it does imply that the buffer stock must start the period with initial commodity reserves in order to always have stocks at nonnegative levels.

The presumed knowledge of the real secular price trends tends to reduce the costs and increase the profitability of buffer stock pure stabilization operations in comparison to situations in which large errors are made concerning the secular trends. In our simulations, errors are not made because of confusion between short-run and long-price movements. In principle, alternative and perhaps more realistic target pricing rules could be explored with our models: lagged moving averages, fixed prices, and so on. Resource constraints preclude such an investigation in this study. However, Smith [5] conducts some such explorations for the copper market. In that case, he concludes that five-year lagged moving averages (that is, for 1975 the average price in 1970-1974, for 1980 the average price in 1975-1979, and so on) result in too great cyclical fluctuations and give a poor estimate of the trend, with the result that the buffer stock follows some bizarre behavior that causes substantial losses. Much better performance results when the price target is fixed for long periods of time (ten years, for example). Of course, such a rule, like the trend rule used here, can be implemented only with very good expectations about real price movements at the time at which the price is fixed.

The price target and floors and ceilings are in real terms. This choice is made because economic behavior generally is posited and empirically tested in real terms (see Chapter 3 and Appendix A). In the absence of money illusion, moreover, long-run equilibrium prices also are in real terms, and the aim of pure price stabilization schemes is to limit fluctuations around long-run real equilibrium prices. Note that the use of price targets in real terms is not the same as indexing—that is, assuring that the price of such commodities does not change relative to some other prices, such as those for the imports of the developing nations. The secular trend in the real price may be either up or down.[7] The directions of movement reflect changes in the long-run market forces.

The prices, and all other variables in the model, are annual averages. The use of these annual averages may understate somewhat the costs of buffer stock operations. Buying and selling transaction costs may be incurred during a year in which the buffer stock both buys and sells because otherwise the price would move above and/or below the allowable range, and yet the average price would be within the allowable range (thus indicating no transaction costs). This problem probably is more important for agricultural products with strong seasonal cycles, such as cocoa. For actual operation in such cases, a seasonal component might usefully be superimposed on the secular trend to avoid too many transactions that would be reversed shortly thereafter in the same crop year.

The bandwidths around the secular price trends that are maintained by the buffer stock operations in the simulations are ± 15 percent. The choice of bandwidths is important. Credible narrow bandwidths increase price stability, but they destroy future markets[8] and some of the motive for private

---

7 Section 5.4 explores the implications of efforts to change that trend. Indexing is a special case in which the secular trend of real prices is changed to zero.

8 A future market is one in which a person can make a commitment in the present to provide or to acquire a commodity at a specified price at some future date. For example, on July 1, 1979 I might make a commitment to sell 3000 tons of copper at a price of $3.00 a kilogram on June 30, 1980. I presumably would do so only if I thought that I could acquire this amount of copper before then at a price sufficiently lower than $3.00 to make it profitable to make the future commitment. Future markets exist for a number of commodities, including some of those of interest in this study. Look in a major newspaper and you can find the daily prices of buying or selling in these markets for delivery at specified future dates.

If the price bands are too narrow and are credible, operations in such future markets may not be expected to be profitable. Smith [5] reports on interviews with future traders in the New York copper market which indicate that they could still operate profitably with ± 10 percent bands, but it would not be easy.

inventories, as well as reduce (perhaps to large negative numbers) profits from the buffer stock operations since such profits depend primarily on price differences between buying at the floor and selling at the ceiling. Broad bandwidths do not stabilize prices much. The choice of a narrower bandwidth for some alternative simulations should give some insight into the sensitivity of the results to the choice of the bandwidth.

Finally, it should be emphasized that the simulated rules of operation that we use for the buffer stock are quite simple and mechanical. Buffer stock managers might well have more information than is included in these simulations. More flexible rules of operation might be desirable.[9] To the extent that either of these possibilities is true, the mechanical procedure simulated here may overstate the costs of buffer stock operations.

4. The net cost of a buffer stock operation is the sum of three components: (a) the cost of the initial commodity stock (if any);[10] (b) the net value of all activities (that is, revenues minus expenditures) of the buffer stock during the decade; and (c) the value of the buffer stocks still held at the end of the decade. Revenues are from sales at the price ceiling (with a constant percentage discount in cases where it is necessary due to quality deterioration, such as for coffee). Expenditures are from purchases at the floor price, transaction costs (a constant percentage of sales or purchases), storage costs (a constant rate for the average stocks held each year), and stock deterioration (at rates proportional to quantities). All rates and ratios (that is, for transaction costs, storage costs, price, discounts, and deterioration) are assumed to be constant in real terms at levels suggested by UNCTAD [6]. The initial and final stocks are valued at the average prevailing market prices in the year before and year after the decade of buffer stock operation.

The question of how to evaluate dollars spent or received at different points of time raises two issues. The first is in regard to how to treat price movements over time. If all prices double between 1978 and 1985, for example, then in an important sense a dollar received (or spent) in 1985 is worth only about half as much as a dollar received (or spent) in 1975. As is indicated in the previous paragraph, we can deal with this situation by putting

---

9 An example of a more flexible rule would be to shift the price band (or perhaps the floor or the ceiling) inversely with the size of the buffer stock. Such a procedure would enable the buffer stock managers to adjust their behavior in light of the information which they received about the underlying basic supply and demand shifts from the changes in the buffer stocks. However, it also might increase uncertainty for the private sector and reduce price stability.

10 This initial commodity stock, as is indicated above, is just of sufficient magnitude to allow the buffer stock operations to always defend the ceiling over the decade of the simulation.

all of our prices and values in real terms. That is, we can correct by an index of overall price movements so that our prices and values are in terms of the purchasing power of a common base year. In the present case, we use 1975 as the base year. Therefore, to obtain prices and values for other years in terms of real 1975 dollars, we adjust for the movements in the overall price index. To continue the above example, a dollar in 1985 would be worth only 50 cents in 1975 prices if the overall price index doubled in the intervening decade.

But that still leaves a second issue about comparing values and prices over time. Even after we have corrected for overall price movements, there is a difference between receiving a dollar this year and a dollar at some time in the future. Ask yourself: If you knew that you would be alive and healthy in a year and that there would be no price changes in the next year, would you rather receive a dollar now or one year hence? If you were to receive a dollar now, you could put it into a savings account and receive interest on it for a year. With a 5 percent rate of interest, for example, if you received a dollar now and put it into a savings account, you would have $1.05 in a year. Therefore, even if prices were constant and there were no chance that you would not be able in a year to enjoy the use of whatever funds you were to have then, a dollar now is preferable to a dollar in a year.

Now let us change the question slightly: Under the same conditions as in the previous paragraph, what is the minimum that you would be willing to receive in lieu of receiving a dollar a year hence? The approach to answering this question should be clear. Let X be the unknown amount that is the minimum you would be willing to receive now. With an interest rate of 5 percent, in a year X will be worth $X*$ (1.05). For you to be indifferent between receiving X and $1.00 in a year,

$$X*(1.05) = \$1.00. \tag{5.1}$$

The solution to this relation is:

$$X = \$1.00/1.05 = \$0.95. \tag{5.2}$$

For values smaller than this, you would be better to borrow at the interest rate of 5 percent and pay back your debt plus interest a year hence with the dollar you would receive then.[11] Therefore, the amount that would leave

---

11 Consider, for example, a value of 90 cents. If you borrow 90 cents now at five percent interest you will have to pay back 90 * 1.05 = 95 cents in a year - which you could do with the dollar which you were to receive then if you elected that option, and still have five cents left.

you indifferent between receiving it now and the alternative of $1.00 in a year is $0.95. In other words, the present value of receiving a $1.00 in a year is $0.95 now if the interest rate is 5 percent. Usually this value is referred to as the present discounted value, since it is the present value of an amount to be received in a year given the interest or discount rate. In the more general case in which the discount rate is r, the present discounted value of a dollar to be received in one year is $1.00/(1 + r)$.

Now let us test your understanding. Under the conditions indicated above, what is the present discounted value of receiving a dollar two years hence? First ask yourself, what is the value one year from now of receiving a dollar in two years? By analogy with the above discussion it should be clear that the answer is $0.95 = \$1.00/1.05$—or $1.00/(1 + r)$ in the more general case. Then the question reduces to: What is the present discounted value of receiving $0.95 (or $1.00/(1 + r)$ in one year? By the same process, the answer is $0.91 = 0.95/(1.05) = \$1.00/1.05)^2$ (or $1.00/(1 + r)^2$ in the general case). By extension you should realize that the present discounted value of receiving a dollar five years hence is $1.00/(1.05)^5 = \$0.78$ and for n years hence is $1.00/(1.05)^4$ (or $1.00/(1 + r)^4$ in the general case).

Now that we have explored these two important issues concerning the evaluation of prices and monetary values over time, let us return to the net value of the buffer stock operation. To represent this real net value, we want to measure all components in real terms and use present discounted values of all of the components so that they are comparable. We therefore focus on the present discounted value of buffer stock operations in 1975 prices, using a 5 percent real discount or interest rate.

Now let us turn to another critical issue in estimating the present discounted value of buffer stock operations over a decade. What is the real present discounted value of any stocks held at the end of the decade? An upper limit can be obtained by calculating the real present discounted value if they were sold at the prices that actually prevailed in the year after the decade (1973). But this clearly is an upper limit, since any effort to sell them then would drive down the prices in that year. A lower limit can be obtained by assuming that they have no value. Reality presumably is somewhere between these two limits. We focus on this lower limit below in order to come up with a conservative estimate of the net value of buffer stock operations.

Concluding Comments about Assumptions

We could ask a lot of questions about our assumptions similar to this question about how we evaluate buffer stocks that are still held at the end of the decade. Some of these we explore in the simulations by comparing the results of two simulations that are identical except for a specified change in a particular assumption. In this way, we examine the sensitivity of the results to the particular assumption, so such a process is called sensitivity analysis. How do we decide which sensitivity analyses to conduct? The answer of economists is to explore those cases for which the value of the expected additional insight is at least as great as the expected additional cost.

We are not able to explore all of our assumptions by sensitivity analysis, however, because of the substantial cost that would be required to explore every possible alternative. Nevertheless, in order to emphasize the fact that our simulated results do depend on a number of assumptions, we list some of the possible biases in our simulated values of the real present discounted values of buffer stock operations.

The impact of some of the assumptions underlying the simulations is to overestimate the present discounted net value of the buffer stock programs. These assumptions are that private stocks do not fall due to less incentives for hedging and speculating on upward price movements, that the greater price certainty does not cause shifts in the supply function or increase its elasticities or shorten the supply lags within the decade, that the price ceilings can be defended even though the buffer stock starts with just sufficient quantities to assure nonnegative levels during the decade of operation, that historically operative production and export restrictions on the commodities of interest are not changed, that the secular price trends are known by the buffer stock operators, that in a given year for a particular buffer stock there is not both selling and buying, that initial stocks are valued correctly at 1962 prices, and that storage costs do not increase with the increased volume. Other assumptions, which probably result in an understatement, are that private stocks do not increase due to less incentives for hedging and speculating on downward price movements, that the greater price certainty does not result in greater private inventories and/or greater demands with shorter lags due to risk aversion, that the buffer stock managers have no better information than that described by the mechanical rules of behavior that are utilized in the simulations, that no additional export or production restrictions are imposed, that storage and transaction costs do not exhibit economies of scale, and that the final stocks have no value.

To a certain extent, or course, these biases are counterbalancing. If one or the other dominates, however, it is my judgment that the present discounted values probably are overestimated (in other words, the *costs* of the buffer stocks are understated). In any case, the major point of this partial list of possible biases due to our assumptions is to ensure that readers should not overemphasize the exactitude of our simulation estimates. They depend critically on our assumptions. We hope that by rooting our analysis in economic theory and historical experience, we have a firm foundation for our analysis. Nevertheless, a large number of assumptions underlie the results and not all of them can be explained by sensitivity analysis at a reasonable cost. Therefore, the simulation outcomes should be interpreted as suggestive orders of magnitudes, not exact dollar amounts.

5.3 SIMULATIONS OF BUFFER STOCK PRICE STABILIZATION FOR UNCTAD CORE COMMODITIES AND BASIC FOODGRAINS

The first major goal of most international commodity agreements, including the UNCTAD program, is to stabilize the prices of a number of commodities (see Section 2.2). For many of the commodities of concern in the UNCTAD proposal, historical price and revenue fluctuations have been considerable (see Section 4.1).

We now apply the general procedures outlined in Subsection 5.1.3 to simulate the effects of international buffer stock programs to stabilize prices for the 1963-1972 decade within a 15 percent band of long-run secular trends. We consider eight [12] of the UNCTAD core commodities and two major foodgrains: coffee, cocoa, tea, rubber, jute, sisal, copper, tin, wheat, and rice. These simulations are conducted under the assumptions that were discussed in detail in the previous section.

Table 5.2 summarizes the most pertinent output of these simulations. For each commodity, Table 5.2 gives the average annual percentage changes in price, quantity, and producers' revenues; the maximum buffer stock required over the decade; the longest continuous period of buffer stock activity without buying and without selling; the present dicounted value in millions of 1975 dollars of additional producers' revenue due to stabilization (with a 5 percent real discount rate, see point 4 in Section 5.2); a measure of revenue stability in the ratio of the standard deviation [13] of real producers' revenue with stabilization to that without stabilization; and the present discounted values in millions of 1975 dollars of buffer stock operations, excluding and including the value of final stocks (with a 5 percent real discount rate). The point of all comparisons is a base simulation that is identical to the simulation with the buffer stock except that there is no buffer stock activity. Column numbers refer to Table 5.2 unless otherwise indicated.

---

12 Sugar and cotton are not included because of problems in developing satisfactory models.
13 The standard deviation is a measure of the variation around the average value. The smaller it is, everything else being equal, the more closely bunched around the average are the values. It is defined as the square root of the average of the squared deviations from the average. For example, the following two series have the same average of 100: (a) 150, 50, 170, 190, 10, 30, and (b) 101, 99, 97, 96, 100, 107. The respective standard deviations are : (a) 71.9 and (b) 3.6. The latter series clearly is more closely bunched around the average and has the smaller standard deviation.

Table 5.2 Summary of simulations of buffer stock price stabilization schemes for eight of UNCTAD core commodities and two basic foodgrains*

Commodity	Mean percentage changes as compared to base simulation			Maximum buffer stock (1000 Metric tons)†	Longest continuous period (in years) of buffer stock activity		Present discounted value of real revenue: stabilization-base simulation, millions of 1975 dollars at 5% real discount rate	Ratio of real revenue standard deviation in stabilization/base simulation	Present discounted value of buffer stock activity, millions of 1975 dollars at 5% real discount rate	
	Price	Quantity supplied	Value of producers' revenues		Without buying	Without selling			Excluding final stock	Including final stock
	(1)	(2)	(3)	(4)	(5)	(6)	(7)	(8)	(9)	(10)
UNCTAD core commodities										
Coffee	4.7	0.6	5.2	21738†	5	7	2662	1.0	-4	324
Cocoa	10.0	1.2	11.1	546†	4	10	1115	0.5	-126	351
Tea	0.8	0.1	0.9	161	8	9	114	0.9	-5	243
Rubber	9.2	0.0	9.2	3432	7	4	2243	0.5	-879	777
Jute	0.0	0.0	0.0	0.0†	10	10	0.0	1.0	0.0	0.0
Sisal	8.9	0.5	10.2	232	5	5	-1	0.4	-53	-16
Copper	-0.9	0.0	-0.9	507	7	2	-1339	0.8	-730	-454
Tin	-5.2	-1.0	-6.2	19	10	1	-656	0.9	-95	-95
Core commodities (sum or average)	3.4	0.2	3.7		7.0	6.0	4140		-1892	1130
Basic foodgrains										
Wheat	0.1	0.1	0.2	1200	4	7	0.0	0.9	-2997	-1865
Rice	11.1	0.5	11.8	1600	3	3	33440	1.0	-5054	-641
Basic foodgrains (sum or average)	5.6	0.3	6.0		3.5	5.0	33440		-8051	-2509

*Details of the underlying econometric models are given in Adams and Behrman [1], Agosin [2], and Behrman [3]. The buffer stock simulations are identical to the base simulation except that the buffer stock purchases or sells whatever is necessary to keep the deflated price within the indicated band-width of the secular trend for 1963-1972 decade. The simulations are all for the 1963-1972 decade. The initial and final stocks are valued at the 1962 and 1973 prices, respectively, which overstates the present discounted values of buffer stock operations. For discussion of other assumptions, procedures, and biases, see Sections 5.1 and 5.2.

†Units are: thousands of 60 kg. bags for coffee; thousands of long tons for cocoa; millions of pounds for jute.

These statistics are the basis for a number of important observations about the operations of commodity buffer stocks. All of these comments, of course, are conditional on the assumptions outlined above (a qualification that, for economy of space, is not constantly repeated). We focus on the UNCTAD core commodities because the results suggest that the food-grains should be treated separately (see point 7 below). Here we concentrate on the aggregate results. The next chapter considers some of the disaggregate implications.

1. The gross revenue gains to the developing countries from the operation of these specific programs may be large. The increase in the present discounted value of real producers' revenues exceeds 4 billion 1975 dollars for the eight core commodities included (column 7).[14] This present discounted value is equivalent to a constant value of 536 million 1975 dollars per year over the decade. Weighting the present discounted value of real gross revenue gain for each commodity by the share of developing country production of that commodity (Table 6.1) gives a total of 5.4 billion dollars to the developing countries for the eight core commodities, which is equivalent to a constant annual flow over the decade of 700 million real dollars per year. Note that the developing countries' gain exceeds the total gain. How can that be so? The answer is that the developing countries have relatively high proportions of the world production for those commodities with simulated positive gross revenue gains (for example, coffee, cocoa, and rubber).

Are these gains to the developing country producers substantial? It depends on the point of comparison. Relative to the values implied by changing the secular trend (see Section 5.4) or the $65 billion per year implied by OPEC operations in oil, they are not large. In comparison to existing governmental flows from developed to nonpetroleum exporting developing countries, however, they are not insignificant.

From where does this revenue gain to the developing country producers come? In part, it reflects negative present discounted values of buffer stock operations (column 9). The division of the sources of financing for these sources depends on the exact details of the negotiated agreements—but at least a portion of the funds probably would come from the developing countries themselves. The origin of the largest part, however, is increased expenditure on the sum of these commodities by consumers, who are concentrated in the developed countries. (See Table 6.4 for the percentage distribution of imports among country groups).

---

14 If the UNCTAD estimates of the proportions for the purchase cost of sugar and cotton to that of the other eight core commodities can be used as a guide, the figures for the eight core commodities for which simulations are presented need to be multiplied by a factor of 1.5 to 1.7 to obtain estimates for all ten core commodities.

With perfect knowledge, therefore, the motivation for the advocacy of these specific buffer stock schemes for the core commodities by the developing countries as a group, *ceteris paribus*, is clear.

In the same situation the opposition by informed consumers is clear unless they see the transfer of resources to commodity producers as desirable and unobtainable by other means or unless they see the large possible gains for themselves due to the lessening of inflation pressures (see point 10 below). Of course, consumer interests are not always well represented in such negotiations because they are diffuse. Governments of consumers may agree to such arrangements because they think that transfers to the developing countries are desirable. Explicit direct transfers, however, are politically unpopular among their constituents—who, on the other hand, would not perceive well the nature of the transfers if they were through increased prices. To be more explicit, the International Coffee Agreement that Fisher [7] suggests transferred 500-600 million dollars per year may have had such a character. There was no large organized consumer opposition to the agreement. Yet it is not obvious that the governments of the consuming nations could have proposed alternative additional direct transfers of the magnitude involved to the coffee-producing nations without substantial political opposition.

2. The gross revenue gains vary substantially across commodities. For the specific programs and conditions examined, the present discounted real values of revenue gains to coffee, cocoa, and rubber total over six billion dollars. The same statistic for copper and tin is about *minus* two billion dollars. These differences are due primarily to differences in where the no-buffer stock price path was in 1963-1972 (due to the underlying supply and demand forces) relative to the secular trend for the 1950-1974 quarter century.

Under different conditions or with different rules of operation the details would change, but a dispersion of gross gains probably would remain. The variance of gains across the producers of different commodities would seem to cause real strains in any integrated program. There would be producers who would perceive themselves (perhaps correctly) to be losers. How would they react? Unless they were reimbursed somehow by the gainers (which would seem unlikely), why would they continue in the program? These are difficult questions indeed for the integrated program.

3. Revenue does not seem to be destabilized by these programs. As Section 3.1 discusses, price stabilization by buffer stock operations may or may not stabilize revenues. Under the assumptions of these simulations, revenue fluctuations remain the same for most commodities but are reduced for cocoa, rubber, sisal, and perhaps tin, tea, and copper (column 8). Everything else being equal, the general stabilizing effects of the agreements on prices and in some cases on revenues would make them desirable from the point of view of risk-averse producers and consumers.

4. The present discounted net cost of the buffer stock agency operations depends critically on the evaluation of terminal stocks (and on other assumptions), but may be quite considerable in absolute value. The present discounted net cost of buffer stock agency operations without including the value of terminal stocks is − $1,892 million for the eight core commodities (column 9). The exclusion of sugar and cotton, in addition to the biases discussed above, suggests that these estimates are probably too high (algebraically). In other words, the losses probably would be greater.

But in one respect these figures are biased downward, perhaps considerably: terminal stocks are valued at zero. If terminal stocks are valued at the post-terminal-year market price, in fact, for many of the individual commodities and for the sum of the eight core commodities, the present discounted values are positive (column 10). However, such a calculation is misleading, since (a) the post-terminal year's (1973) actual prices generally were quite high (and presumably would not have been anywhere near as high if such programs had been in operation for 1963-1972 and had accumulated buffer stocks), and (b) stocks could not be sold in the post-terminal year without driving down the price. Under the assumption that there are no other sources of bias, a comparison of columns 9 and 10 leads to the conclusion that for nonnegative present discounted values of buffer stock operations the terminal stock must have been salable in the post-terminal year at least at 63 percent of the actual price prevailing in 1973 on the average for the eight core commodities. Sales at such prices seem unlikely. When consideration is given to other biases, moreover, it appears to be almost certain that the present discounted net costs of buffer stock operations for most of these commodities (but perhaps not for coffee, jute, and tea and for the sum for the core) are negative.

Does a negative value for buffer stock operations mean that they are undesirable? From the point of view of all producers combined together the answer is no. Net gains are positive even if the losses due to buffer stock operations (with final stocks valued at zero) are subtracted from the gross revenues (column 7-column 9): $2,248 million for the eight core commodities.

What about the broader viewpoint? Smith [5] argues that a necessary condition of an optimal buffer stock operation (one that maximizes the sum of consumer and producers' surpluses; see Section 3.2) is that its expected present discounted value is zero. However, such a rule is not optimal if there is risk aversion or if there are distributional effects. Both of these considerations raise the possibility that a socially optimal policy implies negative present discounted values. If that is the case, then subsidies are required to follow such a policy.

5. The choice of price bandwidths affects substantially the orders of magnitude involved. Going from a ± 15-percent band to a ± 5-percent band around the secular price increases gross present discounted producers' revenues from $4,140 million to $5,851 million and reduces the present discounted value of buffer stock operations — $1,892 to — $4,141 million for the sum of the eight core commodities. For every individual commodity and for the sum, the present discounted value of buffer stock operations (ignoring terminal stocks) is reduced. Fluctuations in real revenues are reduced fairly substantially for tea and wool and somewhat for rubber, jute, sisal, and copper. However, they are increased substantially for wheat and somewhat for coffee and tin.

Because of the larger magnitudes involved in the buffer stock operations, the negative effect on private stockholding and future markets, and the better signals provided by somewhat larger price variations, the ± 15-percent bandwidths are more relevant that the ± 5-percent possibility for most, if not all, of the commodities of interest.

6. The results also are somewhat sensitive to the discount rate. Going from a 5- to a 2-percent *real* discount rate, for example, increases the present discounted real values of gross producers' revenue from $4,141 to $4,856 million and of buffer stock operations from − $1,892 to − $2,333 million for the sum of the eight core commodities. Such differences are of some consequence. However, of much more significance than this range of discount rates are questions related to the bandwidth and the evaluation of terminal stocks.

7. The simulations reinforce other information that suggests that the basic foodgrains should be treated separately from the core commodities. In the original UNCTAD proposal, in addition to the ten core commodities, a number of other products—including rice and wheat—are mentioned. The orders of magnitude in the simulations are higher for the grains than for the core products involved. For example, the real present discounted value of buffer stock operations in rice and wheat (ignoring final stocks) is − $8 billion as compared to − $1.9 billion for the eight core commodities (column 9). The inclusion of these grains would increase drastically the overall financial requirements. This result reinforces other considerations (for example, humanitarian concerns about limiting starvation) that led to the exclusion of these grains from the final UNCTAD integrated commodity resolution.[15] For wheat, furthermore, production and exports are much less concentrated

---

15 As noted in Section 2.2, they were included explicitly in the UNCTAD [8] proposal, but not in the UNCTAD IV [9] resolution.

in the developing nations (Table 6.1). For these reasons we focus on the core commodities here.[16]

8. *The dynamic lags suggest that there may be long periods without selling or without buying, that agreements should cover a number of years, and that the financial requirements are spread over several years.* The lag structures, especially in the production of the tree crops and of the minerals, imply fairly long supply adjustments in a number of cases. For several of these products, for example, supply increases in response to initial price rises drive down prices after six or seven years. The dynamics of the supply and demand interactions also cause long periods in which particular buffer stocks do not buy or do not sell: 7.0 and 6.0 years respectively are the averages across the eight core commodities (columns 5 and 6). The implications are several: (a) If there is no selling for a long period of time most of the agricultural stocks have to be rotated, which increases transaction costs and lowers the present discounted value (or increases the cost) of buffer stock operations. (b) The possibilities of fairly long swings make it difficult to separate the cycle from secular trends and, therefore, to know if inventories are too large at a particular point in time. This characteristic makes it difficult to know how to trigger export and production quotas. Quotas have the effect of limiting buffer stock acquisitions, but have shortcomings because they may disrupt capacity expansion, cannot defend the price ceiling unless applied on use or imports, and are difficult to allocate. They also have been opposed by the United States on the grounds that they artificially limit supplies (Katz [11]). (c) Likewise, the judgment of the success or failure of a particular agreement is difficult to make until it has operated for a while. (d) For most, if not all, of these commodities, therefore, it would seem preferable if agreements were longer than the five years maximum suggested by the Havana Charter (see Section 4.3) and followed since then. For this to be possible, the agreements probably have to incorporate a fair amount of flexibility. (e) Also, for most agreements the highest financial requirements are not at the start, but only after stocks build up over several years. In the extreme case of tea, for example, no purchases are made until the ninth year. Therefore, the required funding will not be used all at once, but over a number of years.

9. *The access to financial resources of six billion dollars suggested by UNCTAD is not likely to be sufficient for the core commodities.* We are assuming that the financial reserves of any buffer stock are sufficient so that its intention and ability to maintain the price floor is credible to speculators. Evaluating what this means is difficult. However, we can obtain a

---

16 For extensive investigation of proposed programs for foodgrains, see Sarris, Abbott, and Taylor [10].

lower bound for the sum of all eight of the core commodities by asking how much would be required to purchase the maximum stocks implied by the simulations (column 4). We evaluate those quantities at the average 1970-1974 prices, which is the most conservative choice among the three alternatives considered by UNCTAD [12, 13]. The answer is $5,085 million, which is 75 percent greater than the UNCTAD estimate for the same eight commodities at the same prices. And even this answer is low for at least two reasons additional to the difficult question of what reserves are required to convince speculators of the capability to define the price floor: (a) Finances are needed for transactions and storage costs, not only for acquisitions. (b) This calculation is based on the average nominal 1970-1974 price, which probably is too low due to general inflation. Changing to the average real 1970-1974 price would increase the value by 27 percent to $6,473 million.

If the same proportional adjustments are made to the UNCTAD estimates for sugar and cotton, the total is about $10.4 billion. And this still does not include backup reserves to guarantee success against downward speculation. Therefore, we must conclude that the proposed fund probably would be inadequate for the conditions of our simulation.

The UNCTAD [8] proposal and the UNCTAD IV [9] resolution base their estimates in part on the use of a common fund for financing. To the extent that fluctuations are out of phase across commodities, the common fund allows a reduction in the total required financing. We turn to this topic in the next chapter.

10. Gains from the reduction of inflationary pressures, especially for consuming nations, may be substantially greater than the revenue gains to producing nations or the cost of buffer stock operations. To this point we have focused on the implications of the proposed buffer stock arrangements within the framework of the operations of the relevant commodity markets. Within that framework the simulations suggest that a fairly substantial resource transfer may occur from consumers to producers.

However, from a broader perspective it is possible that consumers would reap much larger benefits, given inflation-output tradeoffs. Over the quarter century ending in 1975, the ten core commodities had average price levels substantially above the secular trends a number of times: in twenty-seven cases there were prices from 15-30 percent above the trend, in eighteen cases 30-50 percent above, in nine cases 50-100 percent above, and in four cases over 100 percent above. These commodity prices high above their trends may cause inflation that is not reversed when the commodity prices subsequently decline. Let us consider this possibility.

We start by asking: What is the magnitude of the impact of commodity price rises on inflation in the developed countries? Popkin [14] estimates that a 14.5-percent increase in the price of nonfood and nonfuel raw materials causes a 1-percent increase in the consumer price index of the United

States. The LINK world econometric model[17] suggests that a 33-percent increase in prices of nonfuel commodity exports from the developing countries is required to increase the consumer price index of the United States by 1 percent (Waelbroeck [15]). The latter is an underestimate of the impact of changes of international commodity prices on inflation in the United States because it considers only the effect of the proportion of commodities that are produced in the developing countries. Both estimates are on the low side to the extent that there exist substantial oligopolistic industries that use commodity price rises to implement "cost-justified" increases in their own prices, as Cooper and Lawrence [16] have hypothesized. On the other hand, both estimates are high for our purposes to the extent that they include more commodities than the ten that are in the UNCTAD core group. Nevertheless, they suggest that as a conservative ball-park range, increases of 30-60 percent in the prices of the core commodities would be required to cause a 1-percent rise in the United States consumer price index. In conjunction with the history of commodity price increases summarized above, such a range suggests that imposing $\pm$ 15-percent bands on prices might reduce inflationary pressure at least by 0.2 to 0.4 percent in the United States, for several years in a decade of operation.

Such numbers *prima facie* may not seem to be so large. But what do they mean in terms of real output? To answer such a question we must first introduce the notion of the tradeoff between inflation and unemployment that is illustrated in Fig. 5.3. The vertical axis gives the percentage increase in prices or the rate of inflation. The horizontal axis refers to the unemployment rate. The curve indicates that lower unemployment is associated with more inflation and vice versa. For example, a move from point *a* to point *b* in Fig. 6.1 is associated with a reduction in inflation from 7 to 5 percent, but at the cost of increasing unemployment from 6 to 7 percent—roughly one million individuals. Now what increase in unemployment would be required to avoid the price increase of 0.2 to 0.4 percent to which reference is made above? The available empirical estimates of the inflation-unemployment tradeoff suggest an addition in the unemployment rate of 0.03 to 0.3 percent.

We are nearing the end of our quest for an answer. We now need only to translate this unemployment rate into output. Okun's [17] Law, based on empirical estimates, suggests that output falls about 3 percent for every 1-percent increase in the unemployment rate. This implies that the 0.03- to 0.3-percent required increase in unemployment is translated into about 0.1

17 The LINK project consists of a series of interconnected or linked econometric models of the national economies in the world. Each of these models is estimated by techniques similar to those mentioned in Subsection 5.1.2 and is simulated under various assumptions much as we are doing here.

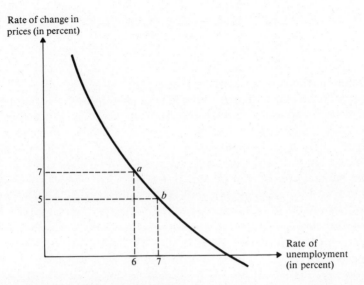

Fig. 5.3 Inflation-unemployment tradeoff

to 0.9 percent of real GNP. To be conservative, consider the middle of this range. It implies a gain of about $8-9 billion 1975 in one year for the United States economy! Let us continue to be conservative by assuming that such years occur only twice in a decade. The present discounted value of the gain to the United States economy over the decade would be about $15 billion. In addition, similar gains would be experienced in other developed market economies.

Such an estimate is only a ballpark figure based on assumptions about price-employment-output tradeoffs and on rough estimates. Nevertheless, it suggests the possibility that the really large gainers from international commodity stabilization programs may be the residents of the developed nations due to the amelioration of inflationary pressures. Of course, there also would be some similar, although probably smaller, benefits to the producer countries because of the reduction of worldwide inflationary pressures.

5.4 SIMULATIONS OF BUFFER STOCK PROGRAM TO INCREASE THE SECULAR PRICE TRENDS FOR THE UNCTAD CORE COMMODITIES AND THE BASIC FOODGRAINS

The second major goal of the UNCTAD program and resolution is to increase real revenues for the developing country producers of a number of internationally traded primary commodities (see Section 2.2). For many of these commodities, secular trends in real prices and, in some cases, in real revenues have been negative over the last quarter century (see Section 4.2).

We now apply the general procedures outlined in the previous chapter to simulate the impact of using international buffer stock programs to maintain prices for the 1962-1973 decade within a 15-percent band of a secular trend for which the annual growth rate of deflated prices is 2 percent above that actually experienced in the last quarter century. That is, instead of using the secular trends in Table 4.2, we add 2 percent algebraically to each of those estimates (so that the trend for the deflated price for coffee grows at −1.5 percent instead of −3.5 percent for example). As a result, the secular trends are 10.5 percent above the ones implied by the estimates in Table 4.2 in the fifth year and 22.1 percent above in the tenth year. This is tantamount to indexation if the actual trend is −2.0 percent, but less (more) than indexation if the actual trend is below (above) this rate. The other assumptions underlying these simulations are identical to those discussed in Section 5.2 above. Table 5.3 summarizes these simulation results.

A comparison of the results in Table 5.3 with those in Table 5.2 leads to a simple observation: The changes implied are enormous! For the sum of the eight core commodities the gross real producer revenue gain as compared to the base simulation is $87 billion instead of $4 billion. The equivalent constant annual value is $11 billion instead of a little over a half billion. The present discounted real value of buffer stock operations excluding final inventories (which must be valued at close to zero in this scheme, given their sizes) is −$12 billion instead of −$2 billion. The maximum buffer stocks at least double and generally increase by a factor of five or more. The average longest continuous period of buffer stock activity without selling is 9.5 instead of 6.0 years. For the basic foodgrains the orders of magnitude are even larger, with present discounted values in 1975 dollars of 429 instead of 33 billion for the additional producers' revenues and of −203 instead of −8 billion for the cost of buffer stock operations.

The producers of these commodities obviously would be very happy with such arrangements. And, while the numbers mentioned are quite large, for the eight core commodities the real producers' average annual revenue gain is only about a sixth of the transfer due to OPEC petroleum prices (or a quarter if an adjustment is made to include cotton and sugar). From such a perspective, these numbers are not all that large.

On the other hand, the costs to consumers are quite substantial—although, once again, much smaller than for the OPEC experience. Therefore, the appropriate conclusion seems to be that to alter the secular trend of the deflated commodity prices by much for very much time implies changes and commitments of orders of magnitude that probably are economically and politically infeasible. This is true whether such an effort is intentional as part of an international agreement or is accidental due to incorrect perceptions of the secular price trend by the buffer stock managers.

Table 5.3 Summary of simulations of buffer stock programs to keep real deflated price within 15 percent of trend—2 percent greater than actual secular trend for a decade*

Commodity	Mean percentage changes as compared to base simulations			Maximum buffer stock (1000 Metric tons)†	Longest continuous period (in years) of buffer stock activity		Present discounted value of additional real revenue due to program (billions of 1975 U.S. Dollars) at 5% discount rate	Present discounted values of buffer stock activity, millions of 1975 dollars at 5% discount rate	
	Price	Quantity	Value		Without buying	Without selling		Excluding final stock	Including final stock
	(1)	(2)	(3)	(4)	(5)	(6)	(7)	(8)	(9)
1. Core commodities									
Coffee	45.9	2.0	48.5	104822†	3	10	23	-394	11110
Cocoa	57.4	3.7	63.0	2552†	0	10	7	-1077	3110
Tea	47.5	7.2	59.0	2611	3	10	10	-1032	5695
Rubber	50.7	8.3	64.1	20526	0	10	22	-4748	11913
Jute	28.5	5.6	35.8	2893†	1	10	2	-640	-141
Sisal	67.4	8.1	82.9	1124	3	10	2	-332	-27
Copper	27.4	1.1	28.7	5578	1	6	20	-3732	9006
Tin	19.1	2.1	21.7	40	0	10	2	-73	238
8 core commodities (sum or average)	43.0	4.8	50.5		1.4	9.5	87	-12028	40904
2. Basic foodgrains									
Wheat	50.3	10.9	67.3	604730	0	10	171	-147385	-55068
Rice	63.3	6.3	73.9	112280	3	10	258	-55941	-10063
Foodgrains (sum or average)	56.8	8.6	70.6		1.5	10	429	-203326	-65131

*The details are the same as for the simulations summarized in Table 5.2 except that the trend of reference for the deflated real price in column 1 of Table 4.2 is augmented by 0.02.

†Units are: thousands of 60 kg. bags for coffee; thousands of long tons for cocoa; and millions of pounds for jute.

Such a result means that attempts to increase the secular trend even slightly will probably be under great strain. Considerations of the theoretical and historical factors underlying successful producer oligopolistic collusion to increase prices (Sections 3.4 and 4.3), moreover, suggest that in some dimensions the conditions for success with the core commodities are present (for example, product homogeneity, frequent transactions, a common perceived interest), but in many others they are not for all or many of the commodities (for example, high fixed costs and scale returns except possibly for the minerals). For none of the ten core commodities do all of the desirable conditions seem to be present. For none of the ten core commodities, therefore, is successful imitation of the OPEC producers' cartel very likely.

Therefore, the possibility of maintaining such price-increasing efforts even for a little while probably increases substantially if the governments of the consuming countries can be persuaded to cooperate. Such cooperation may enforce discipline and limit the expansion of fringe producers. This probably is a basic reason that the developing countries have proposed international commodity agreements instead of producer associations.

This basic result, together with the fairly long swings noted in the previous section, also points to the great difficulty of operating a price stabilization agreement. Short-run fluctuations must be separated from long-run trends for such an agreement to be successful. If not, it will not add much to stabilization or it will absorb large resources (or sell everything) attempting to maintain a too high (low) secular trend. And historical experience suggests that identifying the underlying trends is indeed difficult.

5.5 CONCLUSIONS

The simulation mode of analysis is a powerful tool to supplement the theoretical and historical analyses of the previous two chapters. It is particularly useful in cases in which the phenomenon under examination is complex, with simultaneous and lagged feedbacks and nonlinear responses. We first have reviewed three major steps in performing simulations: model specification, model estimation, and model simulation. We also have made explicit the assumptions underlying our simulations of international buffer stock commodity agreements.

Then we have simulated the general aggregate characteristics of the operation of such agreements for most of the UNCTAD core commodities and for basic foodgrains. The simulations reinforce other considerations that suggest that the foodgrains should be treated separately, so we focus on the former group. Our results suggest that there are possible problems with such agreements, such as the large financial magnitudes involved if the secular trends of the commodity prices are overestimated. They also suggest that in the aggregate the gains may be significant for the developing producing economies. Also, there may be even larger gains from price stabilization agreements for the developed economies, given the inflation-output trade-off. Therefore such agreements at least seem worth exploring from the points of view of both consumers and producers.

REFERENCES

1. F. G. Adams and J. R. Behrman. *Econometric Models of World Agricultural Commodity Markets: Cocoa, Coffee, Tea, Wool, Cotton, Sugar, Wheat, Rice.* Cambridge, Mass.: Ballinger Publishing, 1976.

2. M. Agosín. "Preliminary Econometric Models of Sisal, Iron Ore, Rubber, and Copper." New York: UNCTAD, 1976.

3. J. R. Behrman. "Mini Models for Eleven International Commodity Markets." Philadelphia: University of Pennsylvania (report for UNCTAD), 1975.

4. UNCTAD. "A Common Fund for the Financing of Commodity Stocks: Amounts, Terms and Prospective Sources of Finances." Geneva: UNCTAD, 1975.

5. G. W. Smith. "An Economic Evaluation of International Buffer Stocks for Copper." Houston: Rice University, 1975.

6. UNCTAD. "Progress Report on Storage Costs and Warehouse Facilities." Geneva: UNCTAD, 1975.

7. B. S. Fisher. *The International Coffee Agreement: A Study in Coffee Diplomacy.* New York: Praeger, 1972.

8. UNCTAD. "An Integrated Commodity Programme." Geneva: UNCTAD, 1976.

9. UNCTAD. "Resolution Adopted by the Conference: Integrated Programme for Commodities." Geneva: UNCTAD, 1976.

10. A. H. Sarris, P. Abbott, and L. Taylor. "The New International Economic Order: World Grain Reserves." Washington, D. C.: Overseas Development Council, 1977.

11. J. L. Katz. "International Commodity Policy." Statement by Deputy Assistant Secretary for Economic and Business Affairs before the House Subcommittees on International Organizations; International Policy; and International Trade and Commerce. Washington: 1976.

12. UNCTAD. "A Common Fund for the Financing of Commodity Stocks." Geneva: UNCTAD, 1974.

13. UNCTAD. "A Common Fund for the Financing of Commodity Stocks: Amounts, Terms and Prospective Sources of Finances." Geneva: UNCTAD. 1975.

14. J. Popkin. "Commodity Prices and the U.S. Price Level." *Brookings Papers on Economic Activity* 2, 1974.

15. J. L. Waelbroek (ed.). *The Models of Project Link*. Amsterdam: North-Holland Publishing, 1976.

16. R. N. Cooper and R. Z. Lawrence. "The 1972-1975 Commodity Boom." *Brookings Papers on Economic Activity* 3:671-715 (1975).

17. A. M. Okun. *Proceedings of the Business and Economics Statistics Section, American Statistical Association*. (1962).

International 6
Commodity
Agreements: the
Integration and
Distribution Aspects

In the previous chapter we discussed the overall general characteristics of simulations of price-stabilization and price-increasing buffer stock programs for the UNCTAD core commodities and for basic foodgrains. On the basis of these overall results, we have tentatively concluded with a qualified endorsement of exploring further such programs, from the point of view of both producers and consumers.

But there also are important questions on a less general level that should be considered in evaluations of international commodity programs. We now turn to two of these: What are the advantages, if any, of having an integrated program such as advocated by UNCTAD, instead of separate arrangements for each of the commodities? What nations would benefit and lose from the institution of these programs? The first two sections of this chapter consider these two questions. Then conclusions are presented.

6.1 ADVANTAGES OF INTEGRATION

In the period before World War II, most attempts at commodity market control were undertaken in isolation with little attempt to transfer insights gained from experiences in one market to another. However, the 1935 London conference and several League of Nations conferences provided for increasing interchange about commodity market problems. In the postwar period the United Nations facilitated still greater interaction. A further development in this evolution is the recent UNCTAD emphasis on integrated commodity programs. Section 4.3 provides further detail about these historical trends.

The UNCTAD IV resolution is entitled an "Integrated Programme for Commodities" (Section 2.2). It refers to the possibility of multiproduct commodity agreements as well as individual agreements ("measures to be applied singly or in combination") and attempts to set a timetable for negotiations of a whole group of commodities. The most explicit form of integration implied by the resolution is to explore the possibility of a common fund, which would provide integration of financing for various commodity agreements, not necessarily integration of operations. Until very recently the United States generally has opposed integration on the grounds that the problems in various commodity markets are so particular to those markets that there is not a useful basis for the adoption of common procedures (for example, see Katz [1]). It is not clear that this objection should apply to the establishment of a common fund.

This history leads to the question: What are the implications of integration, particularly in the form of a common fund? UNCTAD [2] argues that the existence of price cycles that are out of phase across commodities implies that merging of financial requirements lowers the total requirements, that merging reduces risks, that the common fund would permit exploration of agreements for commodities in cases in which the producing countries are in sufficient short-run financial straits that they would be unable to support their share of an isolated commodity arrangement, that merging may lead to better terms in international capital markets, and that the existence of such a common fund will serve as a catalyst for the negotiation of commodity agreements. We now consider empirical evidence that applies to some of these issues.

One relevant question is to what extent have the deflated commodity prices of interest moved together? The more closely they have moved together, the less there is the possibility of reducing risks or of lowering the total required funding by having an integrated program.

A measure of how two series move together is provided by a correlation coefficient. If two series move exactly together, the correlation coefficient between them is 1.0. If they move exactly in opposition (for example, one goes up 10 percent when the other goes down 10 percent), the correlation between them is $\div 1.0$. If they tend to move neither together nor in opposition, the correlation coefficient is close to zero.

Table 6.1 gives the correlation coefficients for the 1954-1972 period among the deflated prices for the UNCTAD core commodities. If you understand the notion of a correlation coefficient then you should understand why the diagonal elements are one in this table and why it is not necessary to present the entries both above and below the diagonal. Among the 45 correlation coefficients for the prices of the ten core commodities, only fourteen are significantly different from zero and positive. The other thirty-one, of which fifteen are negative, are not significantly different from zero. That is, the probability is greater than 1 in 20 that they could be as different from zero as in Table 6.1 purely by chance even though there is no real associa-

Table 6.1 Correlation coefficients among deflated prices for UNCTAD core commodities for 1954–1972*

Price		1	2	3	4	5	6	7	8	9	10
Cocoa	1	1.00									
Coffee	2	0.00	1.00								
Tea	3	0.65	0.80	1.00							
Sugar	4	0.41	0.53	0.42	1.00						
Cotton	5	0.76	0.92	0.81	0.63	1.00					
Rubber	6	0.46	0.55	0.82	0.44	0.70	1.00				
Jute	7	−0.15	−0.04	0.35	−0.11	0.03	0.33	1.00			
Sisal	8	0.19	0.23	0.40	0.68	0.42	0.50	0.25	1.00		
Copper	9	0.09	0.12	−0.10	−0.28	0.09	−0.11	−0.30	−0.34	1.00	
Tin	10	−0.44	−0.24	−0.31	−0.37	−0.36	−0.42	0.03	−0.06	0.39	1.00

*Data Source: See Table 4.2.

tion in the movements of the relevant deflated prices. The negative correlations all involve jute, tea, or copper.

That less than a third of the historical correlations among the UNCTAD core commodity prices are significantly positively correlated does support the case for financial integration. Because correlations are less than perfectly positive, diversification lowers the overall risk. When one deflated price is falling, not all others tend to be declining at the same time. The lower risk could lead to better terms in the capital market.

The less than perfect correlations among fluctuations across commodities also have implications for the size of the capital fund to which an integrated financing scheme need have access in comparison to a set of individual funds. Table 6.2 provides some estimates germane to this question: year-by-year values of stock purchases and sales for each of the eight core commodities for which simulations are given in Table 5.2. A first glance at these estimates might temper optimism about the extent of reduction in financial requirements due to integration under the assumptions described above. Among the eight core commodities over the decade, the absolute value of transactions that opposed the dominant trend in a given year (that is, buying when the sum of the eight core commodities sold or vice versa) averaged only 3 percent of the absolute value of all transactions. From this point of view, the gains from integration in terms of reducing capital requirements seem small.

However, such a view is quite narrow. If, instead of focusing on the funding for each year in isolation, a broader and more dynamic view is taken, the possible gains seem to be substantial. For example, the sale of

Table 6.2 Value of simulated buffer stock annual purchases and sales in millions of United States dollars over decade of operation with ± 15-percent bonus around secular trends in deflated prices*

Commodity	Year of buffer stock operation									
	1	2	3	4	5	6	7	8	9	10
Core Commodities										
Coffee	1048	0	0	0	46	0	0	-1210	-0	0
Cocoa	65	0	141	29	19	0	0	0	0	91
Tea	0	0	0	0	0	0	0	0	193	-0
Rubber	0	0	0	-6	-2	-0	0	1	693	627
Jute	0	0	0	0	0	0	0	0	0	0
Sisal	-2	-4	-3	-2	-1	1	5	7	7	7
Copper	95	33	-29	-92	-64	-201	-158	-43	-3	219
Tin	0	-1	-4	-8	-14	-18	-15	-8	-4	-2
Sum of 8 core commodities	1206	28	105	-79	-16	-218	-168	-1253	886	942

*From simulations summarized in Table 5.2.

copper and tin in the third through ninth years could finance much of the purchases of coffee and cocoa in that period. And the large sale of coffee in the eighth year could cover much of the purchases of cocoa, tea, rubber, and copper in the next two years. Thus in a dynamic respect, there are gains from integration in the sense that funding from sales of one commodity could concurrently or subsequently be used to purchase another. This consideration, therefore, might reduce the total required funding for price stabilization for the ten core commodities below the $10 billion estimate in Section 5.4.

But let us think a little bit further. Does it really require an integrated fund to capture these gains? If a country were a financial subscriber for each of the ten individual commodity funds, could it not do this pooling on its own without the common fund? The answer is yes. For countries that are supporting all or most of the commodity agreements, possibly including the United States, there is no gain to pooling finances across commodities by the integrated fund as opposed to doing their own financial pooling. However, for financing of countries that would be liable to be involved in only one or a few of ten individual agreements, such as most of the developing country producers, pooling on their own is not such an easy option. For their finances, the integrated fund is liable to provide an advantage in pooling across commodities.

The price-stabilization simulations in Section 5.3 also point to another aspect of integration. Under a given set of conditions in a given time period, some commodity producers may gain from stabilization and others may lose. Under the assumptions made in the previous chapter, for example, producers of coffee, cocoa, rubber, and, to a lesser extent, tea are the gainers. Producers of copper and tin are the primary losers. The former group could compensate the latter and still come out ahead. But such compensation is not explicitly included in the current UNCTAD IV resolution. Without such compensation the losers probably would soon drop out of the arrangement, which would destroy the integrated effort. The gainers, therefore, might want to compensate, but be resentful of any transfers that seemed to represent overcompensation. In a world of imperfect information and uncertainty, tensions over such compensation may make it very difficult to maintain an integrated arrangement.

Finally, let us consider what is quite possibly the major underlying (although not always explicit) motive for the proposed integrated commodity agreements: the hope on the part of the developing countries that such a scheme will enable them to wrestle more control over commodity markets from the developed nations than otherwise would occur. Since UNCTAD is a largely developing-nation-dominated international organ, an integrated scheme developed under UNCTAD auspices likely would be sensitive to developing countries' interests. The integrated nature of the scheme, in these hopes, would lead to greater relative bargaining power for the developing countries by joining common interests collectively across commodities, would increase the bargaining power of the developing countries for commodities for which their position is weaker by association with the stronger cases, would increase the probability of funding from such sources as OPEC, and would ensure that commodity agreements were explored in cases desirable from the point of view of developing countries, but not so much so from the point of view of the developed nations. The last possibility would include commodities for which the developing producers have sufficient aggregate power to force some redistribution of benefits to themselves in producer-consumer nation bargaining, but not enough power to create a producer cartel on their own.

These possibilities are difficult to evaluate. Examination of the empirical data, however, does lead to an observation relevant to integration of a somewhat speculative nature, but perhaps of quite important significance. Table 6.3 gives concentration ratios and the Herfindahl-Hirschman concentration indices for the ten core commodities. Concentration ratios give the percentage of production (or exports or imports) accounted for by the four (or eight) largest participants. The higher the concentration ratio, everything else being equal, the greater the market power. The Herfindahl-Hirschman indices are the sum of the squares of the shares of each of the participants, and probably give an even better indication of the degree of concentration of power. The higher are these indices, the greater is the indicated concentration. In the case of monopoly (or monopsony) they equal one.

Comparison of the Herfindahl-Hirschman indices for exports and imports suggests that exports are more concentrated for seven of the ten commodities. Generally, bargaining power increases with concentration, *ceteris paribus*.[1] This pattern suggests that exporters might have more power than importers in the bilateral oligopolistic bargaining for commodity agreements on a one-by-one basis.[2]

---

1 Sometimes, however, the opposite may be the case. For example, it has been argued that the developed nations agreed to the transfer of resources through the coffee agreement in the 1960s in part because it was politically expedient precisely because so many developing nations export coffee. Furhtermore, the apparently relatively greater producer bargaining power in the case of coffee than for some other commodities with higher concentration indices may be due to the lack of *ceteris paribus* conditions. For example, higher income levels might make it possible for some producers to restrict exports more easily in this case than for some other commodities.

2 Of course everything else is not equal. Diaz-Alejandro [5] in fact suggests that there is such inequality in bargaining explicitly between the developing and the developed nations that the former might be better generally to avoid commodity agreements since the negotiation thereof requires bargaining in a bilateral framework.

Table 6.3 Indices of concentration by countries for production, exports, and imports of UNCTAD core commodities

	Production in 1972-1973*			Exports in 1970-1972†			Imports in 1970-1972†		
	Concentration ratios‡		Herfindahl-Hirschman index	Concentration ratios‡		Herfindahl-Hirschman index	Concentration ratios‡		Herfindahl-Hirschman index§
Commodities	4 Countries	8 Countries		4 Countries	8 Countries		4 Countries	8 Countries	
	(1)	(2)	(3)	(4)	(5)	(6)	(7)	(8)	(9)
Core commodities									
Coffee	43	64	.07	56	71	.13	63	76	.17
Cocoa	73	87	.16	76	100	.19	55	73	.10
Tea	65	75	.20	77	92	.22	51	63	.11
Sugar	32	47	.03	54	71	.13	60	72	.13
Cotton	63	81	.12	48	67	.08	38	57	.07
Rubber	84	93	.26	90	96‖	.33‖		65	.04
Jute	98	100	.47	81‡	81‡	.29‡	38	47	.07
Sisal				65	76**	.11**	59	75**	.13**
Copper	56	80	.10	70	90	.14	63	82	.13
Tin	66	89	.14	79	94	.23	63	80	.14

* Calculated from data in Jiler, et. al. [3]. The year is 1973-1974 for coffee and 1967 for jute.

† Calculated from data in UNCTAD [4].

‡ The percentage share accounted for by 4 and 8 leading countries.

§ The sum of the squares of the shares. The fewer the number of participants and the larger the share of the dominant producer the higher is this index. For a monopolist or monopsonist, it is one.

‖ Seven countries only.

\# Three countries only.

** Six countries only.

But what happens with integration? If all the commodities are considered as a group, this conclusion well may be reversed. Exports come from a wide range of countries. There are twenty-nine countries represented as one of the four leading exporters of the ten commodities, and only Brazil appears for more than two commodities.[3] Imports go largely to a more limited group. There are only twelve countries included among the four leading importers of the ten commodities. The United States is the leading importer of all but cotton and copper, the Federal Republic of Germany is among the four leading importers in seven cases, and France, Japan, and the United Kingdom appear five times each. The greater the integration in the negotiating process, therefore, the more the shift of effective concentration and therefore probable bargaining cohesion and strength from developing exporting countries to the developed importing nations. This observation may bring into question at least one of the assumptions of the developing nations about the advantages of integration.

6.2 DISTRIBUTION OF BENEFITS AND COSTS FROM BUFFER STOCK PRICE STABILIZATION

Section 5.3 suggests a number of possible overall benefits and costs of stabilization programs. The distributions of these aggregate benefits and costs among countries is of considerable interest to us in evaluating the proposed international commodity market programs. In this section we explore empirical evidence relevant to these important distribution questions.

The distribution of total benefits and costs across countries, however, in most cases depends on the distribution of production (or exports) and of consumption (or imports) of the relevant commodities across countries. Therefore, we characterize these distributions before turning to specific possible benefits and costs.

Table 6.4 gives the percentage distributions of production, exports, and imports among the developing, developed, and centrally planned nations for the ten core UNCTAD commodities and the basic foodgrains. For the core commodities the developing countries dominate exports with almost three-quarters of the total and over half of every commodity. They also account for roughly half of world production (although substantially less than half for sugar, cotton, and copper). The developed countries dominate imports with approximately three-quarters of the total and over half of each commodity. To the extent that international commodity agreements for these ten core commodities affect producers or exporters, therefore, the de-

---

3 Brazil is among the four leading exporters of sugar, coffee, cocoa, and sisal. UNCTAD [4] provides the listing for exports and imports of all ten core commodities.

Table 6.4 Distribution of production, exports, and imports of UNCTAD core commodities and basic foodgrains among developing, developed, and centrally planned countries

	Percentage distribution of production across country groups 1968-1972*			Exports f.o.b., 1970-1972†				Imports c.i.f., 1970-1972†			
				World (millions of dollars)	Percentage distribution			World (millions of dollars)	Percentage distribution		
	Developing	Developed	Centrally planned		Developing	Developed	Centrally planned		Developing	Developed	Centrally planned
	(1)	(2)	(3)	(4)	(5)	(6)	(7)	(8)	(9)	(10)	(11)
Core commodities											
Coffee	98	2	0	2936	98	2	0	3241	6	90	4
Cocoa	100	0	0	759	100	0	0	781	4	78	18
Tea	79-82	11-12	6	713	82	10	8	771	30	61	8
Sugar	21-33	19-30	23-37	2892	70	23	8	2956	19	65	17
Cotton	32-37	23-26	32-37	2669	63	21	16	2859	20	51	29
Rubber	98	2	0	1004	98	2	0	1230	10	62	28
Jute	100	0	0	750‡	88‡	9‡	3‡	810‡	24‡	62‡	14‡
Sisal	100	0	0	179‡	79‡	21‡	0‡	196‡	7‡	87‡	7‡
Copper	37-42	40-46	10-11	4594	54	40	6	4744	6	87	7
Tin	70-82	6-7	9-11	770	81	16	3	761	12	81	7
All core commodities	45-52	20-27	19-21	17266	74	20	6	18349	12	74	14
Basic foodgrains											
Wheat	11-13	38-40	33-47	3913	4	83	13	4287	42	33	25
Rice	54-55	7	37-38	1222	36	42	22	1215	79	13	7

*The first number refers to production by major producers. The second includes residual production that is distributed across country groups in proportion to the distribution by major producers. The years are 1969-1973 for coffee and rubber; 1966-1970 for jute; and 1967-1971 for copper. The statistics are calculated from data in Jiler, et. al. [3]. The row for all core commodities refers to the distribution of value of production.

†Calculated from data in UNCTAD [6].

‡Includes manufactured products. Breakdown among country groups based on 1972 alone.

veloping countries are most affected. To the extent that they affect importers of these ten commodities, the developed nations are most affected.

For the foodgrains the situation is basically reversed. The developed
economies dominate exports, with over 70 percent of the total export value
for wheat and rice. The developing countries account for over half of the
value of imports, with the rest roughly evenly divided between the developed and the centrally planned groups. Therefore, policies in the international foodgrains market that affect exporters affect primarily the developed nations. Those that have an impact on imports affect the developing
nations most.

Another aspect of the distribution question that has received considerable attention is the nature of the distribution among the developing countries. Tables 6.5 and 6.6 provide some pertinent information for the export
side. Table 6.5 indicates the importance of each of the ten core commodities
and the basic food grains in the export value of fifty developing countries
and concentration indices of these commodities in these countries' exports.
The ten core commodities account for over two-thirds of the export value
for eight countries (in order: Zambia, Mauritius, Uganda, Bangladesh, Rawanda, Chile, Zaire, and Sri Lanka) and over a third for another twenty-
two developing nations (Dominican Republic, Ghana, Cameroon, Sudan,
Guatemala, Bolivia, El Salvador, Haiti, Nicaragua, Togo, Ivory Coast,
Egypt, Malaysia, Ethiopia, Peru, Brazil, Western Samoa, Guyana, Mada-
gascar, Tanzania, Philippines, and Syria). If concentration ratios are used
instead of simply the percentages of export value, as the previous section
suggests may be preferable, the ordering is similar (Zambia, Mauritius,
Bangladesh, Chile, Uganda, Zaire, Sri Lanka, Rawanda, Ghana,...). Thus
the distribution of effects is fairly widespread. The countries affected,
moreover, generally include ones that are not among the more developed of
the developing nations (although there are exceptions, such as Chile).

Table 6.6 gives the distribution of the percentage value of the core
commodity exports that originate in low, medium, and high per capita income countries. The commodities are listed in order of their relative contri-
bution to the low per capita income countries. By this criterion the commodities vary widely: from 97 percent for tin to 11 percent for sugar. For
four of the commodities over half of the benefits to exporters would go to
low per capita income countries. For all of them at least two-thirds of the
benefits to exporters would go to low or medium per capita income countries.

Thus for the ten UNCTAD core commodities (although not particularly
for the foodgrains), programs to benefit exporters would affect primarily
developing economies, often including ones with relatively low per capita
incomes. And yet developing countries with vast numbers of people are relatively unaffected on the export side. Non-OPEC developing countries that
do not have more than a third of their export value in these ten commodities

and that have more than twenty million inhabitants include the People's Republic of China, India (with 20 percent of its exports in the core commodities), Pakistan (13 percent), Mexico (18 percent), Vietnam (although the southern part had 56 percent in rubber in the early 1970s), Burma, Colombia (26 percent), Argentina, and Afghanistan.

The other side of the question about the distribution of effects among developing countries is related to imports and consumption. For the ten core commodities, 12 percent of world imports are by developing countries (Table 6.4). UNCTAD [6] suggests that these are not particularly concentrated in the import basket of a few countries, especially not the poorer ones. Once the basic foodgrains are added, the picture changes drastically. The developing countries account for 42 percent of world wheat imports and 79 percent of world rice imports (Table 6.4). This import dependence again points to separate treatment of these grains.

With this background in regard to the distribution of effects among export-producing and import-consuming countries, let us now turn to a brief listing of the benefits and costs of programs for price stabilization of the core commodities.

1. Gross and net revenue gains and expenditure losses. Section 5.3 explores these magnitudes in detail. Considering all of the core commodities together, the present discounted value of gross net revenue gains to producers is over $4 billion (but remember that there is substantial variance across commodities). Over $5 billion would go to producers in developing countries. The losers are primarily the producers of tin and copper [4] and the consumers of the other core commodities. Most of these consumers and most of the copper producers are not in developing nations. However, the gains from reducing inflationary pressures, which are also discussed in that section (and see point 5 below), may be much larger than these numbers and would go in considerable part to consumers.

2. Reductions in instability. If there are sufficient reserves to preclude excessive speculation, the stabilization programs reduce price instability. The simulations also suggest that, if anything, revenue instabilities are reduced. To the extent that producers or consumers are risk averse, they benefit from less instability. Once again, the former are largely in a subset of developing nations and the latter are largely in the developed countries. For the developing economies a number of spokespersons have claimed that instability is quite detrimental.

---

4 Under other arrangement or other solutions, the producers of some other commodities might lose and those of copper and tin might gain. The point is that probably the producers of some of the core commodities will lose in any given pure stabilization program.

Table 6.5 Average percentage importance and concentration indices for ten UNCTAD commodities and for basic foodgrains in exports of leading developing country producers, 1970-1975*

Commodity: Country:	Total	UNCTAD core commodities											Basic foodgrains	
		Cocoa	Coffee	Tea	Sugar	Cotton	Jute	Rubber	Sisal	Copper	Tin	Concentration index†	Rice	Wheat
Argentina	0											.00		6
Bangladesh	81						81					.66		
Bolivia	50										50	.25		
Brazil	38	2	24		7	5						.06		
Burma	0											.00	38	
Cameroon	53	24	25			4						.12		
Chile	73									73		.53		
China (Rep. of)	4				4							.00		
Colombia	26	5	26									.07		
Dominican Republic	65	8	8		52							.28		
Equador	19		11									.02		
Egypt	44					44						.19	6	
El Salvador	50		38			12						.16		
Ethiopia	40		40									.16		
Ghana	56	56										.31		
Guatemala	50		31		8	11						.12		
Guyana	35				35							.12	8	
Haiti	50		39		8				3			.16		
Honduras	16		16									.03		
India	20			8			12					.02		
Indonesia	13							10			3	.01		
Ivory Coast	44	18	26									.10		
Jamaica	13				13							.02		

*Calculated from data in IMF [7].

†Herfindahl-Hirschman concentration index is sum of squares of shares. The higher the index, the greater the concentration. The maximum value is one.

Table 6.5 (Continued).

Commodity: Country:	UNCTAD core commodities												Basic foodgrains	
	Total	Cocoa	Coffee	Tea	Sugar	Cotton	Jute	Rubber	Sisal	Copper	Tin	Concentration index†	Rice	Wheat
Kenya	28		18	10								.04		
Liberia	13							13				.02		
Madagascar	35		28		4			28	3		15	.08	4	
Malaysia	43				90			28			15	.10		
Mauritius	90				90							.81		
Mexico	18		5		6	7						.01		
Nicaragua	46		14		6	26						.09		
Nigeria	7	6									1	.00	20	
Pakistan	13					13						.02		
Panama	0											.00		
Paraguay	7											.01		
Peru	40		4		8	7				23		.06		
Philippines	34				21	5				13		.06		
Ruanda	73		56									.34		
Sri Lanka	70			52				18			17	.30		
Sudan	51					51						.26		
Syria	34					34						.12		
Tanzania	39		15			14			10			.05		
Thailand	16							10			6	.01	16	
Togo	45	28	15			2						.10		
Trinidad & Tobago	5				5							.00		
Uganda	89		64	5		15				5		.44		
Uruguay	0											.00		
Venezuela	0											.00		
Western Samoa	36	36										.13		
Zaire	71		7							62	2	.39		
Zambia	93									93		.87		

Table 6.6 Percentage shares in exports of the ten UNCTAD core commodities among country groups as defined by per capita income, 1947–1973*

UNCTAD core commodities	Low (under $500)	Medium (between $500 and $1,500)	High (over $1,500)
Tea	97	2	2
Jute	93	1	0
Cocoa	82	16	3
Tin	53	44	3
Rubber	47	53	0
Sisal	40	50	4
Cotton	31	36	28
Coffee	28	64	0
Copper	22	52	27
Sugar	11	67	13

*Adapted from Table III in Michaelopoulos and Perez [8]. Row totals do not sum to 100 because of rounding and because the leading seven to twenty producers do not account for all of the product (but in every case they represent at least 90 percent). The per capita income or product figures are for 1975.

What is the empirical evidence about the impact of instability on real consumption and production decisions? On the consumption side there are no relevant empirical studies for the specific commodities of concern. On the production side the empirical evidence is more extensive. Micro studies are mixed, but indicate some inverse response to risk on the part of developing country producers (for example, Behrman [9], Roumasset [10]). Crosssection macro studies also are mixed. MacBean [11] and Coppock [12] report no substantial association between export instability and the rate of growth or related variables. Kenen and Voivodas [13] report a negative relation between export instability and investment, and Glezakos [14] finds a negative impact on real per capita income growth. Knudsen and Parnes [15] report a positive and significant correlation between export instability and the rate of investment growth and the rate of national product growth. Perhaps the most satisfactory study is the analysis of the world cocoa market and the Ghanaian economy by Acquah [16], which suggests that stabilizing schemes could increase the long-run growth potential in Ghana by limiting cumulative cyclic waves. In general, however, the extent of the detrimental impact of export instability on developing countries remains quite uncertain.

3. Efficient resource allocation. The limitation of price movements by stabilization programs clearly changes the nature of price signals. This has the potential effect of resulting in more inefficient resource allocation. For the bandwidth ±15 percent around the secular trends, however, I doubt for several reasons that a convincing case can be made that price stabilization leads to sufficient inefficiency to oppose it on those grounds alone: (a) The arguments in Section 3.3 (for example, externalities, the theory of the second best) cause grave questions about the efficiency of even purely competitive international commodity markets—which would not exist even without the proposed agreements. (b) The extreme fluctuations experienced historically, in my judgment, are not necessary to give signals for resource reallocation. Sustained prices at one or the other limit and/or sustained buffer stock activity of either selling or purchasing would seem to be sufficient signals. (c) The actual changes in production induced by the simulation of commodity agreements over a decade are not large—a maximum of 1.2 percent for cocoa (column 2 in Table 5.2). With such small changes, resource reallocation presumably is not very great. (d) Other factors (for example, risk aversion, distribution) also need to be considered.

4. Collective action between producers and consumers. Beyond the direct impact of stabilization programs, there might be various indirect motivations of the possible participants. The formation of some commodity control organization might improve information flows to the possible benefit of producers and consumers.

Purchasers might want to ensure access to supplies and be willing to pay somewhat higher prices for more guaranteed availability during production shortages. Among the core commodities, however, only tin is one for which supply access difficulties are even problematical. Therefore, this motive would not seem to be very widespread.

Producers may want to use the forum provided by the price stabilization program to attempt to gain agreement in efforts to increase the secular trend, a subject to which Section 5.4 is devoted.

5. Moderation of inflation. The crude estimates in Section 5.3 suggest that for the United States alone the present discounted value of the gain from reducing inflationary pressures might well be about $15 billion in a decade. Similar calculations would apply to the other industrialized importing nations. The gains to the consumers, therefore, could be quite large in comparison to the transfers to producers mentioned in the first point above. Producers probably also would gain somewhat from the reduced world inflationary pressure.

In summary, the distribution of net benefits may not be ideal under such programs. Given my value judgments, for example, the limited extent to which the large poorer countries would be helped is a definite limitation.

6.3 CONCLUSIONS

Moving from the examination of overall aggregates in the previous chapter to a consideration of their composition gives further insight into proposed international commodity agreements.

Apparently there would be some gain through the reduction in overall financial requirements by the financial pooling that UNCTAD proposes. However, the developing countries might lose somewhat in regard to bargaining power by combining negotiations across commodities rather than having them on an individual commodity basis, if concentration ratios of exports and imports are a guide to relative bargaining power.

Regarding the distribution of benefits, the results are mixed. There may well be a problem of how the gainers among the producers compensate the losers. The limited extent to which some of the large poorer countries would be helped is also a limitation, given my personal value judgments. Nevertheless, there are widespread benefits for large numbers of developing countries, including some of the poorer ones. The consuming nations also may benefit substantially from the reduction of risk and the control of inflationary pressures.

Thus these less aggregate considerations reinforce the qualified conclusion of the previous chapter that international commodity agreements have their shortcomings, but merit serious consideration.

REFERENCES

1. J. L. Katz. "International Commodity Policy." Statement by Deputy Assistant Secretary for Economic and Business Affairs before the House Subcommittees on International Organizations; International Policy; and International Trade and Commerce. Washington, D. C. 1976.

2. UNCTAD. "Progress Report on Storage Costs and Warehouse Facilities." Geneva: UNCTAD, 1975.

3. H. Jiler et. al. (Eds.). *Commodity Year Book 1975*. New York: Commodity Research Bureau, 1975.

4. UNCTAD. "A Common Fund for the Financing of Commodity Stocks: Amounts, Terms, and Prospective Sources of Finances." Geneva: UNCTAD, 1975.

5. C. Diaz-Alejandro. "North-South Relations: The Economic Component." in *World Politics and International Economics*, F. C. Bergsten and L. Krause (Eds.). Washington, D. C.: Brookings Institution, 1975.

6. UNCTAD. "The Impact of Imports, Particularly of Developing Countries." Geneva: UNCTAD, 1975.

7. IMF. *International Financial Statistics*. Washington: International Monetary Fund, 1972-1976.

8. C. Michalopoulos and L. Perez. "U. S. Commodity Trade Policy and the Developing Countries." Washington, D. C.: AOD/PPC (1977).

9. J. R. Behrman. *Supply Response in Underdeveloped Agriculture: A Case Study of Four Major Annual Crops in Thailand, 1937-1963*. Amsterdam: North-Holland Publishing, 1968.

10. J. A. Roumasset. *Rice and Risk: Decision Making Among Low-Income Farmers*. Amsterdam: North-Holland Publishing, 1976.

11. A. MacBean. *Export Instability and Economic Development*. Cambridge, Mass.: Harvard University Press, 1966.

12. J. D. Coppock. *International Economic Instability*. New York: McGraw-Hill, 1962.

13. P. Kenen and Voivodas. "Export Instability and Economic Growth." in *Kyklos* (1972).

14. C. Glezakos. "Export Instability and Economic Growth: A Statistical Verification." in *Economic Development and Cultural Change* (1973). Chicago: University of Chicago Press.

15. O. Knudsen and A. Parnes. *Trade Instability and Economic Development: An Empirical Study*. Lexington, Mass.: Lexington Books, 1975.

16. P. Acquah. "A Macroeconometric Analysis of Export Instability in Economic Growth: The Case of Ghana and the World Cocoa Market." Philadelphia: University of Pennsylvania, unpublished Ph. D. dissertation, 1972.

Conclusion 7

In the past several centuries, a part of humanity has benefited from a sustained economic growth much more rapid than had previously been experienced. But this part of humanity is largely concentrated in the developed nations of Europe, North America, Australia, New Zealand, and Japan.

The majority of humanity has been left in poverty in the poorer nations of the world. Independently of how you value increased economic growth in the more affluent nations, it seems hard to deny that some economic growth or development is required in the poorer lands so that hundreds of millions of persons living there can at least have command over minimal levels of resources that would enable them to rise out of the quagmire of poverty and make some real human choices about their existence.

We do not know as much as we would like about what causes sustained economic growth in the poor lands. But we are able to identify some important factors: accumulation of physical capital, development of human potential, modification of institutions to increase incentives for improvements, and increases in technical knowledge. To induce substantial development clearly requires substantial changes internal to the developing economies.

However, their external economic relations are also important—and represent an area in which the developed countries play a more direct role. At a point in time, international trade can permit a country to consume outside of its production frontier and thus increase economic welfare. Over time, international economic relations can help increase the internal level of well-being by providing more productive inputs and technological knowledge.

In the development decades of the 1960s and 1970s, the developing nations as a whole have had reasonably good economic success—at least in comparison to the experience of the now developed nations at a comparable

118

stage. Nevertheless, frustrations have grown in the developing world. Causes for this increased dissatisfaction include the observations or perceptions that the gap between the developed and developing nations inevitably will increase for decades, that many of the poorest have not benefited from recent aggregate economic growth, that problems of short-run inflation and instability have been increasing, and that the international economic order was created by the more developed countries with their own interests—not those of the poorer lands—primarily in mind.

In the early 1970s the success of the poor oil-exporting nations in raising substantially the price of their petroleum exports and the ensuing controversy served as a catalyst to bind the developing nations together in a call for the establishment of a new international economic order that better accommodates their interests.

At the heart of this call for a new international economic order is the desire for international commodity agreements to stabilize and perhaps to increase the prices of major primary commodity exports of the developing countries. These desires have been systematized in the UNCTAD proposal for an integrated commodity program. Whether or not the details of this proposal are implemented, it seems clear that it has set the framework for much of the debate about international commodity trade in the late 1970s and early 1980s. The outcome of this debate is important for hundreds of millions of persons, including those in the poor producing nations and those who consume coffee, copper, and the other commodities of interest.

There have been a number of analyses and criticisms of the UNCTAD program by policy makers and economists, particularly from the United States. The attitude of the United States government has been one of considerable skepticism, if not outright opposition, especially before the Carter administration. However, most of these analyses have been based on *a priori* reasoning, with little attempt to ensure that the critical assumptions reflect real-world realities.

In this study we have examined the UNCTAD program with three modes of analysis: (1) economic theory, (2) the history of previous related efforts, and (3) simulations with empirically based models of what would happen if the UNCTAD proposal were implemented.

The first mode of analysis suggests that the theoretical objections against the proposal are not firmly based. They depend upon some particular assumptions about the real world, which probably are not realistic. They suggest the need for careful empirical investigations. The theoretical analysis also suggests that there are net gains from international commodity agreements, but that the distribution of these benefits depends on actual characteristics of commodity markets—thus reinforcing the need for careful empiricism.

The second mode of analysis raises questions about the widely accepted belief that international commodity agreements have not been successful. It is true that there is not a lot of evidence of success in price stabilization *per se*. But price stabilization is not the only aim of the proponents of international commodity agreements. Quite possibly more central is the desire to increase prices of commodity exports of the developing countries above the levels they would otherwise have attained. Examination of past history reveals a number of such efforts that were successful in attaining this end for a sufficiently long period of time to have been quite rewarding for the producers. However, it also raises doubts that the producers of the UNCTAD core commodities could successfully do so without the cooperation of the consuming nations, given the characteristics of these markets.

The heart of our analysis is the third mode: simulations of what would happen if the program were implemented for a decade. These simulations use simultaneous dynamic models of the various international commodity markets that are based on the best estimates we could make of the underlying supply and demand relations.

Together with the theoretical and historical inquiries, this simulation approach points to some possible shortcomings of the UNCTAD proposal: the outcome depends critically on how well the buffer stock operators accomplish the difficult task of indentifying the underlying secular price trends; under any given set of conditions the developing country producers of some commodities may lose because of the program even if the developing country producers of all of the commodities taken together gain; some very populous developing countries would not benefit very much; and the access to financing probably required would be one-half to two-thirds more than the $6 billion cited in the UNCTAD proposal. On a more general level, changing the international order does not guarantee that the more important changes internal to the developing countries will come to pass.[1]

These problems are real. They point to some definite shortcomings and the need to qualify any conclusion. Yet in my judgment they are not sufficient to offset some real possible gains to the developing nations. Under the assumptions of our simulations, the developing countries would gain a present discounted value of about $5 billion from the implementation of the price stabilization program and much more if the secular price trends were increased. Among the large gainers are a number of relatively poor countries. The integrated aspect of financing would permit the shifting of funds from one commodity to another over time and create greater credibility regarding the possibility of the agreements defending against speculators. The gains to the developing countries are not liable to be offset by equivalent re-

---

1 Some critics have feared that focus on the international changes may divert attention from important internal changes. On the other hand, if expanded command over resources result from the proposed international changes, they may facilitate internal transformations.

ductions in other net capital flows from the richer lands. And finally, the developed economies also would gain very substantially from the reduction of inflationary pressures.

For such reasons our analysis leads me to a positive, albeit qualified, evaluation of the UNCTAD integrated commodity programme. It should be given very serious consideration by all of the relevant parties. It may have substantial benefits for large numbers of people in all parts of the globe.

Appendix A
Efficiency and Social
Welfare Maximization
under Pure Competition

In Section 3.3 it was asserted that pure competition in international commodity markets leads to efficiency and to social welfare maximization under certain assumptions: the correct initial distribution of input ownership for a given social welfare function, easy entry (for example, due to a lack of legal restrictions and limited increasing returns to scale relative to the size of industries), no externalities, no uncertainty, and pure competition in all other markets. This appendix explores this assertion in somewhat more depth, using simple geometric and algebraic tools.

Let us consider a very simplified world, with all of the assumptions of the previous paragraph. For geometric convenience let us also assume the following: (1) There are two variable production inputs, labor (L) and capital (K), which are available in fixed quantities,[1] and one fixed input, land (T). (2) There are two products, agricultural goods (A) and manufactured goods (M), which may be produced by using capital, labor, and land. (3) There are two individuals, E and F, both of whom gain satisfaction from consuming more A and/or more M.[2] It is convenient to distinguish, as in

---

1 The variable inputs may be shifted between industries. The total amount available is fixed. The fixed input also is fixed in total available supply, but cannot be shifted between industries in the time period under sonsideration.

The assumption of fixed available quantities of variable inputs could be relaxed. Labor, for example, might be supplied at different quantities for different wages, reflecting a leisure-income tradeoff for actual and potential laborers. However, a geometric presentation would become very difficult.

2 If there are only two individuals, it may not be credible that neither has any perceptible impact on market prices. However, each can be thought of as representative of a large number of individuals, each one of which has an imperceptible effect on prices.

Section 3.3, among efficiency in production, efficiency in exchange, and overall efficiency.

EFFICIENCY IN PRODUCTION

Let us first consider the production relations. For each of the two products there is a production relation that gives the maximum number of units that can be produced for each combination of inputs of L and K that are used to produce that product, given the fixed amount of T devoted to that product, existing institutions, and the state of technology.[3] Figures A.1a and A.1b give hypothetical production relations for A and M. Each curve represents the combinations of L and K that can be used to produce the indicated quantity of A or of M, where the increasing subscripts refer to increasing quantities. These curves are referred to as equal-product curves since any one curve gives the varying variable input combinations that can be used to produce a given level of output. The curves are drawn to reflect several assumptions: (1) K and L may be substituted for each other in both production processes; (2) there are diminishing returns so that the additional output obtained by increasing one input while the other inputs are held constant becomes less and less; and (3) the given technologies and endowments of T are such that the production of A is relatively L intensive if the variable inputs are used efficiently (see below).

The purely competitive firm is assumed to maximize its profits, or revenues after paying all inputs, given market prices. Because of diminishing returns to variable inputs and the existence of the fixed input T, the marginal (or minimal additional) cost (MC) for producing one more unit of output is increasing for the typical firm in the agricultural industry (Fig. A.1c). The assumption of pure competition means that a firm cannot perceptibly affect the output price it receives. Suppose, as in Fig. A.1c, that the typical firm in the A industry faces a product price of PA_3. How can it maximize profits? If it chooses to produce and sell less than A_3 units, the price it receives for the last unit is greater than the marginal cost of producing that unit, so profits can be increased by expanding output. If it chooses to produce and sell more than A_3 units, the price it receives for the last unit is less than the marginal cost of producing that unit, so profits can be increased by reducing output. Therefore, the firm maximizes profits when it produces and sells A_3, the quantity for which the marginal cost of the last unit is exactly equal

---

3 Note that we are assuming that the production of A depends only on the marketable inputs purchased and used by A and not on what happens in the M industry. If this assumption does not hold (that is, if there are externalitites in production), pure competition does not lead to efficiency in production.

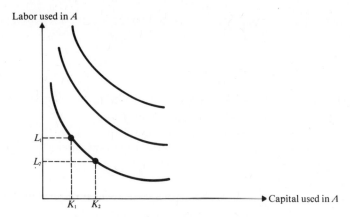

a) Production relations for agricultural goods (A). Possible input combinations for different output levels

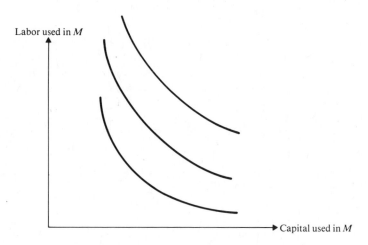

b) Production relations for manufacturing goods (M).
Possible input combinations for different output levels.

Fig. A.1 Production functions and efficiency in production in a two-variable input and two-product world

to the market price PA_3. The general profit-maximizing competitive rule is to produce and sell that output at which the product price equals the marginal costs:

$$PA = MC_A. \tag{A1}$$

We have derived a rule for purely competitive firms to use to maximize profits. But we have not indicated how they chose inputs so as to minimize

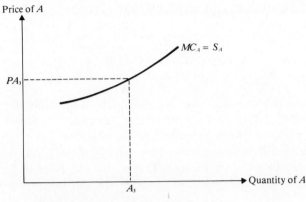

c) Marginal cost and output supply curve for purely competitive firms.

Figure A.1 [continued]

the cost of producing each level of output. If a typical firm in the A sector maximizes profit by producing A_3 units, the question is: what combination of L and K should it elect to use to produce A_3 units? Because the firm is a pure competitor in the input markets, it cannot affect perceptibly the price of labor (PL) or the price of capital (PK) by its decision to hire more or less. Suppose that it selects an input combination where the marginal product of labor (that is, the additional product obtained from adding the last unit of labor) divided by the price paid for the last unit of labor is greater than the marginal product of capital divided by the price paid for the last unit of capital. Then it is obtaining more output at the margin from the last penny spent on labor than from the last penny spent on capital. Therefore, it could reduce costs by buying somewhat more labor and somewhat less capital. Because of the law of diminishing returns, such a shift causes the marginal product of labor to fall somewhat and the marginal product of capital to rise somewhat. Eventually, the marginal products for the last pennies spent on both variable inputs are equalized. Then, and only then, the firm cannot reduce further the costs of producing a given level of output by changing the combination of variable inputs. The cost-minimizing competitive rule is to choose variable inputs so that the marginal products (MP_L and MP_K) per unit cost are equalized:

$$\frac{MP_L}{PL} = \frac{MP_K}{PK}.\qquad (A.2)$$

Alternatively, this rule can be written to say: Inputs should be chosen so that the ratio of the marginal products of the variable inputs is equal to the ratio of input prices:

$$\frac{MP_L}{MP_K} = \frac{PL}{PK}.$$
(A.3)

How does this cost-minimization rule relate to the production relations in Fig. A.1a? Consider what happens when we maintain agricultural output constant at A_1 units, but change the input combination from that at point 1 to that at point 2. The increase in output due to the marginal product of the additional capital $(K_2 - K_1)$ is just offset by the reduction in output due to the marginal product of the lesser labor $(L_1 - L_2)$ so that output remains at A_1:

$$MP_K(K_2 - K_1) + MP_L(L_2 - L_1) = 0.$$
(A.4)

But this expression can be solved for the ratio of the marginal products, which just equals the absolute value of the slope of the equal-product curve for A_1 between points 1 and 2:

$$\frac{MP_K}{MP_L} = \frac{L_2 - L_1}{K_2 - K_1}.$$
(A.5)

Thus, another way of verbalizing relation (A.3) is to say that the cost-minimizing choice of inputs is the one that equates the ratio of input prices to the slope of the appropriate equal-product line.

Of course, all of the same reasoning about profit maximizing and cost minimizing also applies to the purely competitive firms in the M industry.

Now what happens if we consider both industries together? A question of particular interest is: Given the fixed total supplies of inputs L and K and the technical production relations in Fig. A.1a and A.1b, what is the maximum amount of M that can be produced for each level of A? That is, what is the production possibility frontier?

In trying to answer to this question, a bit of geometric manipulation is useful to obtain Fig. A.1d. Begin with the production relations for A in Fig. A.1a. Measure on each axis a distance equal to the total availability of that variable input, and find the point in the plane that represents full utilization of both variable inputs. Now take the production relation for M in Fig. A.1b, rotate it about its origin by 180°, and put its origin on Fig. A.1a at the point that represents the full availability of variable inputs. The result is Fig. A.1d. Each point in this figure represents an allocation of the total fixed supplies of the variable L and K inputs to produce the two products, A and M. Consider, for example, point 1. At that point L_1 units of labor and K_1 units of capital are used to produce A_2 units of agricultural goods, and

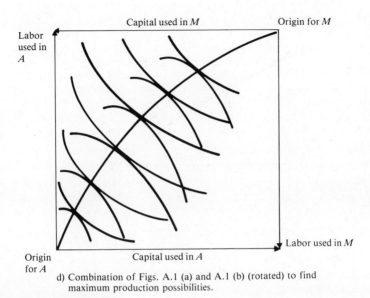

d) Combination of Figs. A.1 (a) and A.1 (b) (rotated) to find
maximum production possibilities.

Figure A.1 [continued

the rest of the available labor and capital are used to produce M_4 units of manufactured goods. Note that the inputs used and the outputs obtained in A production are measured from the lower lefthand origin, but the inputs used and the outputs obtained in M production are measured from the upper righthand origin. Note also that every point in this box represents full employment of both variable factors.

Now we return to the derivation of the production possibility frontier. Consider an output level of A_2 for agricultural goods in Fig. A.1d. Production of A_2 can occur anywhere along the equal product curve for A_2. Examples include the points indicated by 1, 2, 3—and all other points on this equal-product line. Each possible choice of input combinations implies residual inputs for the production of M, which allow M_4 units to be produced at point 1, M_3 units at point 2, M_5 units at point 3, and other quantities at other points. What is the maximum amount of M that can be produced if A_2 is produced? Careful consideration of Fig. A.1d indicates that the maximum is M_5 at point 3. Therefore, the combination of A_2 and M_5 gives us a point on the production possibility frontier in Fig. A.1e.

The same procedure can be followed for every level of A (including levels between those for which equal-product curves actually are drawn in Fig. A.1d) to obtain the whole production possibility frontier in Fig. A.1e. This frontier gives the maximum output combinations that are obtained if and only if all inputs are utilized fully and efficiently. On the frontier, no more

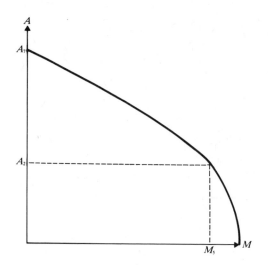

e) Production possibility frontier derived from Fig. 1 (d)

Figure A.1 [continued]

of A can be produced without reducing the quantity of M produced (and vice versa).

How does this relate to pure competition? Think again about how the production possibility frontier is derived from Fig. A.1d. The condition to obtain the maximum level of M that can be produced given a certain level of A is to select the amount of M indicated by the equal-product curve for M that just touches or is tangent to the equal-product curve for the given level of A. But note that every purely competitive firm faces the same input price ratios, so the cost-minimizing conditions in relation (A.3) and the tangency condition in relation (A.5) imply that pure competition leads to this tangency condition! Thus, under the initial assumptions, pure competition leads to efficiency in production and operation on the production possibility frontier.

EFFICIENCY IN EXCHANGE

The theory of consumption is quite parallel to the theory of production. Assume that consumers of E and F have the independent preferences indicated in Fig. A.2a and A.2b, where the increasing subscripts refer to increasing levels of utility or satisfaction. The curves are called equal-utility, equal-satisfaction, or indifference curves because the consumer is indifferent between the combinations of A and M represented by each curve. The shapes of these curves reflect diminishing marginal (or additional) utility as more and more of one good is consumed while the quantity of the other is held fixed.

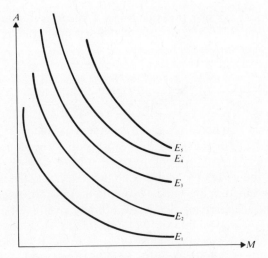

a) Utility or preference function for individual E

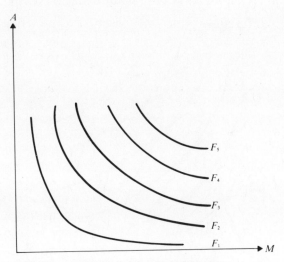

b) Utility or preference function for individual F

Fig. A.2 Utility function and efficiency in exchange in a two-product and two-individual world

Purely competitive consumers are assumed to maximize their utilities given their income and the prices of products. The maximizing condition is that the marginal utilities (MU) be equated for the last penny spent on each item:

$$\frac{MU_A}{PA} = \frac{MU_M}{PM}. \qquad (A.6)$$

The reader should recognize that this rule is analogous to relation (A.2). It can be rewritten as follows: The ratio of the marginal utilities should equal the ratios of product prices:

$$\frac{MU_A}{MU_M} = \frac{PA}{PM}.$$ (A.7)

The reader should also note that, by an argument parallel to that underlying relation (A.5), the lefthand side of this expression is the slope of the indifference curve.

We can combine Figs. A.2a and A.2b (after rotating the latter) for any given level of production of A and M to obtain Fig. A.2c by considerations analogous to those underlying Fig. A.1d. For any given level of satisfaction of individual E, the maximum utility of individual F is obtained by a distribution of A and M between the persons so as to be at the tangency. Fig. A.2d gives a utility possibility frontier, parallel to the production possibility frontier in Fig. A.1e, for the given levels of A and M used in Fig. A.2c.

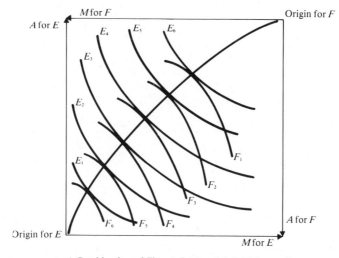

c) Combination of Figs. A.2 (a) and A.2 (b) (rotated)
to find points of efficient exchange

Figure A.2 [continued]

What do we obtain from pure competition? Pure competition in demand leads to satisfaction of the tangency condition. This leads to efficiency in exchange in that no one individual can be made better off without making someone else worse off, given any particular combination of available goods.

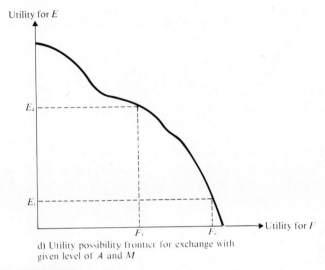

d) Utility possibility frontier for exchange with given level of A and M

Figure A.2 [continued]

OVERALL EFFICIENCY

Production efficiency assures that we are on the production possibility frontier of Fig. A.1e. Exchange efficiency for any given point on the production possibility frontier assures that we are on the utility possibility frontier of Fig. A.2d. But there is a utility possibility frontier like that in Fig. A.2d for every point on the production possibility frontier. Fig. A.3 provides an illustration. To ensure that we are on the grand utility possibility frontier or the outer envelope of these possibilities, the marginal rate of transformation in production (or the slope of the production possibility frontier) must equal the marginal rate of substitution in consumption (or the slope of the relevant indifference curves). The necessary condition is:

$$\frac{MC_A}{MC_M} = \frac{MU_A}{MU_B}.$$

(A.8)

The geometric significance of this condition is illustrated in Fig. A.3b, where the efficiency in exchange condition for A_2 units of agricultural goods and M_5 units of manufacturing goods is drawn inside of the production possibility frontier. Only at point 5 is the above overall condition satisfied. Therefore, in Fig. A.3a only the point corresponding to point 5 in Fig. A.3b on the corresponding utility possibility frontier is on the grand utility possibility frontier.

What about pure competition? Relations (A.1) and (A.7) imply that the marginal rate of substitution (the ratio of the marginal utilities) and the

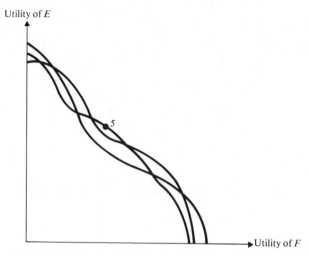

a) A set of utility possibility frontiers, one for each point on the production possibility frontier. Outer envelope is the grand utility possibility frontier

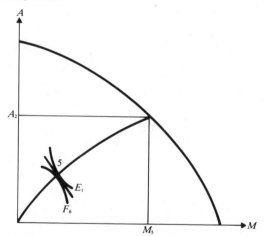

b) Production, exchange, and overall efficiency at point 5 if A^2 and M^5 are produced

Fig. A.3 Overall efficiency and social welfare maximization

marginal rate of transformation (the ratio of marginal costs) are both equal to the product price ratio and thus to each other. Therefore, perfect competition leads to overall efficiency (sometimes called Pareto efficiency), in which no one can be made better off without making someone else worse off.

SOCIAL WELFARE MAXIMIZATION

If we have a social welfare function that depends on the utilities of the different type individuals, we can go one step further. Figure A.3c adds such a function to the grand utility possibility frontier of Fig. A.3a. The condition for maximization, once again, is a tangency condition, such as at point 5. Corresponding to this point is a particular division between individuals of a specific combination of A and M (remember Fig. A.3b). If the initial ownership of inputs is exactly such that the proper incomes are generated, the maximization of a particular welfare function can be attained by a purely competitive system.

Thus, under the assumptions listed at the start of this appendix, pure competition in international commodity markets leads to social welfare maximization. This is a strong result. However, the necessary assumptions also are very strong and are not satisfied in the real world. See the reservations at the end of Section 3.3 for a discussion of respects in which these necessary assumptions are violated in the real world.

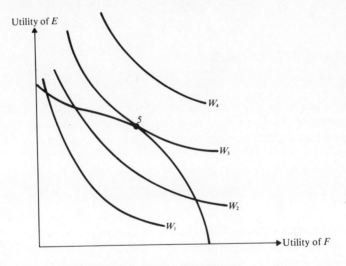

c) Social welfare maximization subject to grand
utility possibility frontier

Figure A.3 [continued]

Appendix B
More Detailed Aspects
of the Methodological
Steps in the Simulation
Analysis

Section 5.1 briefly describes the major steps in the simulation analysis. This appendix provides some more detailed considerations for each of these steps.

B.1 MODEL SPECIFICATION

Supply

The behavior of supply under pure competition is covered in general terms in Appendix A. Now we must be more specific and choose an explicit production function. We choose the most widely utilized form of the production function, the log-linear, constant elasticity, Cobb-Douglass[1] relation:

$$PRO = aL^b K^c e^{rT + sW + u'}. \qquad (B.1)$$

This relation states that production (PRO) depends in a particular way on a set of variables: the inputs of labor (L); capital (K); a time trend (T) to represent secular shifts due to such factors as technological change or the development of irrigation systems for agricultural crops; weather (W), and a disturbance term (u'). The disturbance term is included to represent the effects of excluded variables (such as the impact of pests), of errors in measuring the included variables, and of randomness in human behavior. The other letters (a, b, c, r, and s) are parameters of the function that relate to the impact of the variables on the level of production. These parameters are estimated from real-world data in a manner that is explored in the next section.

---

1 Cobb and Douglas first popularized the use of this function.

We do not dwell long here on the properties of this production function. The interested reader is referred to an intermediate microeconomics text. However, it is useful to indicate that the marginal physical products (that is, the additional product obtained from using an additional unit of an input of labor (MPP_L) and capital (MPP_K)) are:[2]

$$MPP_L = b* \frac{PRO}{L},$$

$$MPP_K = c* \frac{PRO}{K}.$$

(B.2)

We also note that the elasticity of production with respect to labor is the constant b and the elasticity of production with respect to capital is the constant c, for which reason this function often is referred to as a constant elasticity production function. Generalizing from the definition of elasticity given in Section 3.1, the reader should realize that the elasticity of production with respect to an input is defined to be the percentage change in production relative to a given percentage change in an input, everything else held constant.[3]

We now return to behavioral considerations. As is discussed in Appendix A, a profit-maximizing firm with no risk aversion under pure competition selects the output where its marginal cost equals the market price. It also selects a combination of inputs so that the value of the marginal product for each input just equals the price the firm has to pay for that input:

$$PQ*MPP_L = PL,$$

$$PQ*MPP_K = PK.$$

(B.3)

where PQ is the price of the product and PL and PK are the prices of the inputs. For our particular production function in relation (B.1), expressions

---

2 Readers who are familiar with differential calculus may easily verify these relations by taking the partial derivative of PRO in (B.1) with respect to L and K, respectively, and then substituting (B.1) back into the resulting expression.

3 For the reader with some familiarity with calculus, once again, this definition may be written (for L) as:

$$\frac{\delta PRO/PRO}{\delta L/L} = MPP_L * \frac{L}{PRO}$$

Substitution of the expression for MPP_L from (B.2) leads to a value of b.

(B.2) give the marginal physical products for the two inputs. These expressions can be substituted into relations (B.3):

$$PQ*b*\frac{PRO}{L} = PL,$$

$$PQ*c*\frac{PRO}{K} = PK. \tag{B.4}$$

The resulting expressions can be solved to obtain the pure competitor's demand for the two inputs:

$$L = \frac{PQ*b*PRO}{PL},$$

$$K = \frac{PQ*c*PRO}{PK}. \tag{B.5}$$

These input demands, in turn, can be substituted into the production function relation (B.1) and the whole resulting expression solved for the level of production:

$$PRO = a^{1(1-b-c)} b^{b(1-b-c)} c^{c(1-b-c)} \left(\frac{PQ}{PL}\right)^{b(1-b-c)} \left(\frac{PQ}{PC}\right)^{c(1-b-c)} e^{e(rT+sW+u')} \tag{B.6A}$$

This somewhat complicated expression can be simplified by defining a new set of parameters, a_0, a_1, a_2, a_3, a_4 and a new disturbance term u:

$$PRO = a_0 \left(\frac{PQ}{PL}\right)^{a_1} \left(\frac{PQ}{PK}\right)^{a_2} e^{a_3 T + a_4 W + u},$$

$$a_0 = a^{\frac{1}{1-b-c}} b^{\frac{b}{1-b-c}} c^{\frac{c}{1-b-c}},$$

$$a_1 = \frac{b}{1-b-c},$$

$$a_2 = \frac{c}{1-b-c},$$

$$a_3 = \frac{r}{1-b-c},$$

$$a_4 = \frac{s}{1-b-c},$$

$$u = \frac{u'}{1-b-c}.$$

Expression (B.6b) is the supply function for an individual pure competitor. By virtue of the assumption of pure competition, the firm cannot perceptibly affect the price of its product nor the prices of its inputs. But it responds to changes in those prices in order to continue to maximize its profits. If the price of its product (PQ) changes woth everything else (that is, PL, PK, T, W, u, and all the parameters) held constant, for example, the firm increases its production. That is, the supply curve is upward sloping if the quantity the firm supplies is plotted against alternative market prices.

The qualification that everything else is held equal, however, is very important. Such a qualification is behind any supply curve drawn in the product-price versus quantity plane. What happens if everything else is not held constant? Consider, for example, what happens if everything is held constant except that we compare two situations, one with good weather and one with bad weather. For any given market price, the firm produces more when there is good weather than when there is bad weather. Therefore, as is indicated in Fig. 5.2a, the supply curve in the product price-quantity plane *shifts* when the weather changes. At price P_0 with good weather, Q_2 is supplied, but with bad weather, Q_1 is supplied. Similar comments apply for all of the other variables in expression (B.6b). If they change, the supply curve in the product price-quantity plane shifts as is indicated by this expression.

Now let us consider a modification to make our supply relation more realistic. In the real world, many production decisions have to be made without knowledge of what prices will be when the product is finished. For the tree and bush crops (rubber, cocoa, coffee, and tea) that UNCTAD includes in its proposed program, for example, there are lags of two to seven years between the time of planting and the first production.Similar gestation periods exist for the minerals, copper, and tin. Even for the annual agricultural products, at the time of planting producers do not know with certainty what the harvest prices will be a number of months later. Nevertheless, producers have to make decisions. Therefore, we replace the prices in the supply function by the expected prices. The expected prices represent the expectations held by producers at the time of making a decision (for example, whether or not to plant a cocoa tree) regarding the relevant prices at the later time, when the resulting production comes to fruition. But we generally do not have data on price expectations. Therefore we represent these expectations by the weighted average of past prices at the time the decision in question is made.

We should note that often we can distinguish between short-run and long-run supply responses. The short-run response is the response in the current year, or perhaps with a one-year lag, to market prices for a given capacity of production. For example, given a stock of coffee trees a farmer can increase output within certain limits if prices are high by using more pesticides to protect the beans, using more fertilizer to grow more beans per tree, and using more labor so that each picker can be more careful and waste fewer beans. The long-run response, in contrast, is the total response after *all* adjustment have been made. In the long run, no inputs are fixed. More area may be planted with trees, for example. Because of this greater flexibility, responses are generally (but not always) higher and elasticities are greater in the long run than in the short run.

Thus we have developed a specific supply relation for an individual purely competitive producer. To explore the functioning of international commodity markets, however, we need market supply functions. We use supply functions of the general form of relation (B.6b) to represent the aggregate behavior of a large number of producers, each of which behaves in a purely competitive manner. Because of our interest in the three major country groups introduced at the start of this book and because of our belief that the details of such relations may vary across these country groups, in our models we generally include supply functions for the developing countries, the developed economies, and the centrally planned nations. The sum of these three functions gives the total world supply that is indicated in Fig. 5.1.

Demand for Current Use

Demand behavior under pure competition is discussed in general terms in Appendix A. Now we must be more explicit.

We could start with a representation of the utility or preference relation for an individual purely competitive consumer. As is noted in Appendix A, however, the derivation of a demand relation from the maximization of consumer satisfaction for a given level of income and given market price is quite parallel to the derivation of a supply function from the maximization of producer profits for given market prices.

Therefore, rather than derive a demand function here, we posit that per capita demand (D/POP) is a log-linear or constant elasticity function of per capita income or product (GDP/POP); the price of the product in comparison to the price of other consumer goods (PQ/PO); a secular time trend (T) to represent trends in tastes or in technology that affect the use of the product (such as the development and spread of instant coffee or of synthetic rubbers); and a disturbance term (v) that represents the same type of factor as in relation (B.1):

$$\frac{D}{POP} = b_0 \left(\frac{PQ}{PO}\right)^{-b_1} \left(\frac{GDP}{POP}\right)^{b_2} e^{b_3 T + v}. \tag{B.7}$$

The bs are parameters estimated from empirical data. Parallel to the supply relation, $-b_1$ is the constant price elasticity of demand, b_2 is the constant income elasticity of demand, and b_3 is the secular trend.

Other considerations also are similar to those for supply. If the product price changes and everything else is held constant, a downward sloping demand curve is traced out in the price-quantity plane. If other variables like per capita income change, the demand curve shifts in that plane (Fig. 5.2b). To make the model more realistic, we need to represent the creation of price expectations and adjustment processes. Lags of past values are used for these purposes. Similarly, economic theory and empirical evidence suggest that more important than current income per capita in the demand decision is normal, long-run, or permanent income. We represent this possibility by using the weighted average of the income per capita variable for several years, not just for the current year. The introduction of lagged variable values for such reasons again suggests the distinction between short-run and long-run responses or elasticities. Furthermore, we assume that the aggregate demand for current use relation is like (B.7) multiplied by the relevant population variable. Finally, to obtain the total world demand for a particular commodity we once more sum relations similar in general form to expression (b.7) for the developing, developed, and centrally planned economies. This sum is the world demand for current use diagrammed in Fig. 5.1.

Price-Private Inventories

In addition to the demand for current use, there is a demand for net additions (or withdrawals) from private inventories. The determinants of desired private inventories are several. For many products there are discrepancies between seasonal supplies and demand. Most of cocoa production, for example, is in the first quarter of the year for biological reasons, but the demand for chocolate and for other cocoa products is spread out much more evenly over the year. Inventories also may be held to protect the user against supply disruptions due to bad weather or other causes. If there are fixed transaction costs for buying or selling the commodity a profit-maximizing firm also will choose to hold some stocks. Finally, there is a speculative motivation if an individual believes that future prices will be enough higher than current prices to more than cover the costs of holding inventories. The difference between total world demand and demand for current use in Fig. 5.1 is the desired world addition or withdrawal from inventories. In this figure the desired inventory change is negative if current prices are too high. This is based on the assumption that speculators would want to reduce their stockholdings if prices are sufficiently high because they have expectations that future prices will fall to more normal levels.

Actual inventor additions (withdrawals) may be for any or all of these reasons if previous actual inventories were below current desired levels. However, actual inventory additions (withdrawals) may not all be desired. There may be undesired additions (withdrawals) to world year-end stocks (*STK*) if production (*PRO*) exceeds (falls short of) demand for current use

(*D*) and official buffer stock purchases (*BS*). Unless some production is destroyed, the following identity must hold on the aggregate world level (where STK_{-1} refers to the level of private stocks at the end of the previous period):

$$STK = STK_{-1} + PRO - D - BS. \qquad (B.8)$$

In equilibrium this market-clearing relation implies additions to (withdrawals from) stocks of the desired magnitude. Out of equilibrium this market-clearing relation must hold, but actual changes in inventories are not equal to desired changes.

And what happens if actual inventories exceed (fall short of) desired levels? The excess (shortage) put pressure on the market price to fall (rise). Therefore, we postulate a log-linear or constant elasticity world-wide relation between deflated prices (*PDF* = *PQ*/*PO*) and the level of private stocks relative to demand for current use (*STK*/*D*), with a time trend (*T*) to represent secular trends (for example, a reduction in inventory needs per unit of sales as transportation improves) and a disturbance term (*w*) for the reasons indicated previously:

$$PDF = \frac{PQ}{PO} = c_0\left(\frac{STK}{D}\right)^{c_1} e^{c_2 T + w}. \qquad (B.9)$$

The *c*s are parameters estimated from real-world data. To more realistically represent adjustment and expectations formation processes, once again, in actual use we explore the incorporation of lagged values of the included variables. Note that it would be easy to solve relation (B.9) for the private stock level as a function of the deflated price (and perhaps expectations thereof), the demand for current use, a secular trend, and a disturbance term. This would give an explicit relation for desired inventories.

The Complete Model

For reasons of simplicity, let us ignore the breakdown of supply and demand into the three country groupings. Then, in essence, the complete model of any one international commodity market has four relations: a world supply function similar to (B.6b), a world demand for current use function similar to (B.7), the world market-clearing relation in (B.8), and the price-private inventory relation in (B.9). These four relations determine four variables: world supply, world demand for current use, world private inventory additions (withdrawals), and the world price. These variables are called endogenous because they are determined by the system of relations in the model.

Prices link the system because they apear directly or indirectly in all relations. All those relations in which current prices appear are called similtaneous and must be solved together because changes in one affect the others.

If there are any relations with only lagged prices (as is most likely to occur on the supply side since the gestation periods after some critical decisions are quite long) or with no prices, they can be solved separately. Because of the inclusion of lagged prices and other lagged variables to represent the formation of expectations or normal income, adjustments process, and so on, the solution of the model for any period depends in part on the past history of the endogenous variables.

The solution of the model for the four endogenous variables also depends on the magnitude of the relevant parameters (the as, bs, and cs) and on variables that are not determined within the model. This latter group of variables is called exogenous. In this model it includes all prices other than that for the product of interest, weather, the secular time trend, income or gross national product, population, the disturbance terms (u, v, w), and the buffer stock purchases or sales. Changes in any of these exogenous variables affect the solution values for the four endogenous variables, perhaps with a lag.

B.2 ESTIMATION OF THE MODEL

The second step is to estimate the unknown parameters in the model: the as, bs, cs, and characteristics of the disturbance terms. One could obtain these values by a wide range of methodds, including guessing.

What we do is attempt to obtain the "best" possible estimates of these parameters from time series data by what is called ordinary least squares regression analysis[4] (the reason for this name should be clear after you read the next few paragraphs). To understand this process, let us consider a simplified version of the supply function in relation (B.6b) in which the quantity supplied (PRO) is presumed to depend only on the current deflated price (PDF) and the disturbance term (u):

$$PRO = a_0 PDF^{a_1} e^u. \tag{B.6c}$$

This can be transformed into a linear relation by taking the natural logarithms of both sides:

$$\ln PRO = a_0' + a_1 \ln PDF + u, \tag{B.6d}$$

where a_0' is $\ln a_0$.

We have historical data on PRO and PDF for a number of years so we can calculate $\ln PRO$ and $\ln PDF$ for each year. Suppose that we do so and

---

4 We use data over time in this study and the examples in this section also use data over time. The same estimation methodology, however, often also is used with observations across different entities at a point in time.

plot the results in Fig. B.1a. Each point in this figure represents the combination of $\ln PDF$ and $\ln PRO$ observed for that year. That is, for 1972 the particular values of these variables are $\ln PDF_1$, or 1.27 and $\ln PRO_1$, or 4.36.

How can we proceed from this diagram to obtain estimates of the parameters in relation (B.1d)? The most commonly utilized procedure is as follows: Determine the straight line that minimizes the sum of the squares of the vertical distances from each of the observed points to the line.[5] The solid line in Fig. B.1a is an example. The intercept of that line on the $\ln PRO$ axis gives an estimate of a_0'. The slope of the line (that is, the amount by which $\ln PRO$ changes for a given change in $\ln PDF$, or $[\ln PRO_{1976} - \ln PRO_{1975}] / [\ln PDF_{1976} - \ln PDF_{1975}]$ in Fig. B.1a) is an estimate of a_1. The vertical distance from each observed point and the regression line is the estimate of the disturbance term u for that year, as should be clear from relation (B.6d). The estimated disturbance term for 1974, for example, is $\ln PRO_3 - \ln PRO_2$. The estimated values for these disturbance terms are plotted in Fig. B.1b. As this figure indicates, they can be positive or negative, but tend to cluster around a value of zero.

These estimates are best in the sense that they minimize the sum of the squares of the differences between the actual and estimated values of the dependent variable (in this case, $\ln PRO$). That is, they minimize the sum of the squares of the estimated disturbance term. In doing so, they maximize the extent to which the estimated relation is consistent with variations in the dependent variable. No other estimates can be more consistent with these variations by definition. The extent to which any particular set of estimates is consistent with the dependent variable is often summarized by the coefficient of determination, or R^{-2}. This statistic can range from 0 (no consistency) to 1.0 (complete consistency).

Many other complications could be added, but we do not explore them here.[6] However, we have covered the essence of the widely utilized ordinary least squares estimation procedure. This procedure enables us to give empirical life to our theoretical model by incorporating into it the parameter estimates that are most consistent with the real world in the sense described

---

5 We do not worry here about the details of how such a line is determined. For the reader who is familiar with differential calculas, however, the process is not very difficult. Relation (B.6b) is easily solved for u_2 and the result can be used to obtain an expression for the sum of u for all years. Then this expression is minimized with respect to the parameters (a_0' and a_1) by taking the first partial derivatives with respect to these parameters and setting them equal to zero and then solving such expressions for the parameters.

6 Many highly technical books and articles have been written on extentions of this basic procedure to take into account various problems. This subject is called econometrics—the measurement of economic relations.

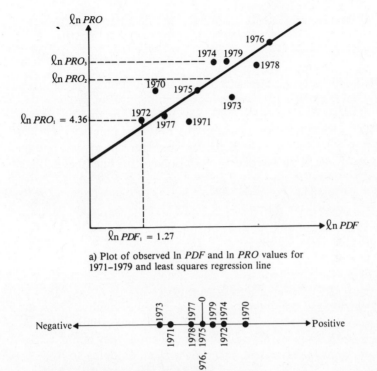

a) Plot of observed ln *PDF* and ln *PRO* values for
1971–1979 and least squares regression line

b) Plot of estimated disturbance terms
(i.e., distances between observed points and regression
lines in Fig. B.1a)

Fig. B.1 Illustration of hypothetical ordinary least squares regression

above. Once we return to our more satisfactory model of the previous
section, of course, we have more than one observable righthand-side variable in each relation. Therefore we have to move from two to more dimensions. Although this increase in dimensions makes diagramatic presentation
very difficult, it in no way changes the basic principle. Ordinary least
squares estimates still are obtained by minimizing the sum of the square of
the deviations from the regression curve in multidimensional space. These
estimates are still the best in the sense that they are the most consistent with
variations in the dependent variable over the period on which they are
based.

   We now turn to illustrations of actual ordinary least squares regression
estimates of the model of the previous section for one of the commodities in
the UNCTAD proposal—cocoa. The relations are the same as expressions
(B.6b, (B.7), and (B.9) with the following exceptions: (1) Lags in various
variables are included to represent the expectational formation and adjust-

ment processes discussed in the last section (subscripts indicate the number of years of each lag). (2) As with the hypothetical example in relation (B.6c) and Fig. B.1, the logarithm is taken before estimation so that the relations are linear (not multiplicative). (3) Because of the lack of adequate data, the price of cocoa is everywhere divided by the same deflator (that from the developed economies) rather that the alternatives indicated in the previous section (*PL, PK, PO*). *PDF* refers to this deflated price. (4) Also because of the lack of adequate data, the weather variable (*W*) is represented not by an actual weather index, but by a variable that takes on a value of one in periods of exception weather and zero in other years. This still causes the entire relation to shift in the price-quantity plane when weather is unusual, as is illustrated in Fig. 5.2a. (5) Some variables in the relations of the previous section are not included in the estimates presented below because initial exploration indicated that they probably are not relevant.

For most commodities, as is indicated in the previous section, the models we use include estimated supply and demand relations for each of the three major country groupings and an overall estimated price-private inventory relation. For economy of presentation here, we give one example of each type for cocoa:

Supply from the developing countries:

$$\ln PRO = -\; 0.024 \ln PDF_{-6} + 0.080 \ln PDF_{-7} + 0.124 \ln PDF_{-8}$$
$$ (0.5) \qquad\qquad (2.0) \qquad\qquad (3.2)$$

$$+\; 0.112 \ln PDF_{-9} + 0.049\, T + 0.041\, W7072 + 0.214\, W65$$
$$ (2.4) \qquad\qquad (7.6) \qquad (1.6) \qquad\qquad (3.0) \qquad\qquad (B.6')$$

$$+\; 6.016,$$
$$(41.4)$$

$$R^{-2} = 0.94,\; SE = 0.061,\; 1956\text{-}1972.$$

Demand for current use in the centrally planned economies:

$$\ln (D/POP) = -\; 0.122 \ln PDF_{-0} - 0.138 \ln PDF_{-1}$$
$$ (2.9) \qquad\qquad (3.1)$$

$$-\; 0.216 \ln PDF_{-2} - 0.150 \ln PDF_{-3}$$
$$(5.1) \qquad\qquad (4.2) \qquad\qquad (B.7')$$

$$+\; 1.18 \ln (GDP/POP) - 7.66,$$
$$(27.4) \qquad\qquad\qquad (37.2)$$

$$R^{-2} = 0.997,\; SE = 0.032,\; 1955\text{-}1972.$$

Price-private inventory relation for world:

$$\ln PDF = -0.858 \ln (STK/D) - 0.026\ T - 0.292,$$
$$\quad\quad\quad\quad (9.2) \quad\quad\quad\quad\quad\quad (5.3) \quad\quad (2.3) \quad\quad\quad (B.9')$$

$$R^{-2} = 0.87, SE = 0.116, 1955\text{-}1973.$$

Before interpreting these results we need to clarify the notation. The variable names are all defined as in the previous section (except that the numbers after the W variable in B.6b' refer to the exceptional years). Before each righthand-side variable is the estimated value of the parameters. For example, in relation (B.9) the estimate for c_1 is -0.858, the estimate for c_2 is -0.026, and the estimate for the logarithm of c_0 is -0.292. In cases in which there are several lagged values of the same variable (PDF in both the supply and demand examples, for instance), the total effect is the sum of the estimated parameters. Underneath each parameter estimate in parentheses is a number that indicates how probable it is that the estimate is actually different from zero. We need not go into details here, but a rule of thumb for these estimates is that a value greater than 2.0 indicates that the odds are only one in twenty that the estimated coefficient actually is not really different from zero. Most of the estimates in relations (B.6b'), (B.7'), and (B.9') are probably different from zero by this criterion. After the estimated relations are three items. The first is the coefficient of determination or R^{-2}, which, as is described above, indicates the extent to which the estimated relation is consistent with variations in the dependent variable. Next is the standard error of estimate (SE), which refers to the sum of the squares of the deviations from the regression line (which is minimized) divided by the number of years. The smaller this number the more closely the estimated values of the disturbance term cluster around zero in Fig. B.1b and the better the relation fits the historical path of the dependent variable. Last is the time period for that estimation.

Now let us consider the individual relations. The R^{-2} for the supply function indicates that the estimated relation is consistent with 94 percent of the variation in ln PRO for cocoa over the 1956-1972 period. There is no evidence of a short-run response to price, but there does appear to be a long-run response in planting cocoa trees. This response occurs after a lag of seven years, due to the biological gestation period between the planting and initial substantial bearing of the cocoa tree. The total long-run price elasticity of supply is 0.34 ($= 0.024 + 0.080 + 0.124 + 0.112$). There also is a fairly large secular trend in production of about 4.9 percent per year, apparently due to technological improvements (such as pest control) and expansion of transportation (such as, the construction of roads, which opened up new producing areas). Finally, there is evidence of a substantial effect of the unusually good weather conditions in 1965, which resulted in an increase of about 21.4 percent in production over normal levels. There also may have been smaller good-weather effects in 1970 and 1972.

The estimated relation for per capita cocoa demand in the centrally planned economies is consistent with almost all of the variation in ln (D/POP) in the 1955–1972 period, with an R^{-2} of 0.997. The estimated long-run price elasticity is -0.626, but the price response is spread out over several years—perhaps because of conscious decisions not to respond too quickly to price changes in order to be sure that they are longer lasting and not ephemeral. The fairly large estimated price elasticity of per capita demand in economies that depend substantially on nonprice allocative mechanisms may be surprising at first. However, it probably reflects a tendency to make a foreign exchange allocation for purchasing cocoa rather than deciding to purchase a given quantity. Thus when the cocoa price goes up, the quantity of cocoa purchased goes down by a fair amount (and vice versa) so that the total foreign exchange expenditures does not vary much. There is no evidence of a secular trend due to changes in tastes. But the estimated per capita income elasticity of 1.18 indicates that average cocoa demand in the centrally planned economies has been increasing faster that per capita product.

The price-private inventory relation in (B.9$'$) is consistent with about 87 percent of the variation in ln PDF in the 1955–1973 period. The first estimated coefficient suggests that the cocoa price is negatively responsive to the level of private cocoa stocks, and positively responsive to the level of demand for current usage. The respective elasicities are -0.858 and 0.858. There also is a negative secular trend of about -2.6 percent per year, perhaps due in part to lessening relative inventory levels for reasons suggested in the previous section.

Thus we have provided illustrations of how to obtain estimates of the basic parameters in the model of an international commodity market such as that postulated in Section 5.1. We do not present further regression estimates here, but we do make use of them in the simulations presented in Chapters 5 and 6, as well as in the discussions in Chapters 3 and 4. In Table 5.1 we present the basic price and income elasticities for the rest of the cocoa model and for the other commodities included in the UNCTAD proposal. All of these elasticities have been estimated from ordinary least squares regressions similar to those we have discussed in this section.

B.3 SIMULATIONS WITH THE MODELS

We will limit additional comments to one distinction that is not made in the texts of Chapters 5 and 6: the distinction between nonstochastic and stochastic simulations. In nonstochastic simulations we assume that the values of the disturbance terms are zero in each year. This is equivalent to assuming that they assume their average value in each year. We then solve for the endogenous variables given all of the other factors noted above. In stochastic simulations we let the disturbance terms have nonzero values. The value for any particular disturbance term in a given year in a simulation is selected randomly from the distribution of alternatives that is suggested by the estimated values of the disturbance term such as in Fig. B.1b or by the standard errors of estimates (SE) discussed in the previous section. By conducting a large number of simulations with alternative values of the disturbance term, we can determine not only the average expected outcome for the endogenous variable but also the extent of variation possible in different alternatives. Some tentative experiments suggest that our results would not be affected substantially by conducting stochastic simulations instead of nonstochastic ones. For reasons of simplicity and cost of calculation, therefore, we focus on nonstochastic simulations in this study.

Index